HUMILITY'S CRY

A Descent into the Heights of God

JORDAN VERNER

WESTBOW
PRESS®
A DIVISION OF THOMAS NELSON
& ZONDERVAN

WestBow Press books may be ordered through booksellers or by contacting:

WestBow Press
A Division of Thomas Nelson & Zondervan
1663 Liberty Drive
Bloomington, IN 47403
www.westbowpress.com
1 (866) 928-1240

ISBN: 978-1-9736-3171-2 (sc)
ISBN: 978-1-9736-3173-6 (hc)
ISBN: 978-1-9736-3172-9 (e)

Library of Congress Control Number: 2018907242

Print information available on the last page.

WestBow Press rev. date: 06/21/2018

DEDICATION

I T IS MY JOY TO DEDICATE THIS BOOK TO MY MOTHER. THE PERSON I am today I trace most distinctly to the many hours of intercession that she sowed on my behalf. I have asked God many times why He sovereignly invaded my bedroom as a seventeen-year-old and changed the course of my life forever. His answer is always the same. It was my mother's prayers. The list can go on and on of times God has reminded me of this truth.

Mom, thank you for laying your life down for me. Thank you for loving me so deeply and selflessly in all the ups and downs of life. The humility you have demonstrated served as a model I have long sought to imitate. Your example in this has been a gift of such high value I lack language to adequately express it. I honor you for the many battles you have won in the prayer closet. My life and this book are the fruits of your victory. Your faithfulness in seeking the Lord has marked me profoundly and set in motion a wake of righteousness that ripples with the redemption of heaven. Your life exclaims, "Only God!"

FOREWORD

PREVAILING WISDOM DICTATES THAT IF SOMEONE WANTS TO MARKET a book successfully, the author and/or the one who writes the foreword should be widely known. In the case of this book, neither its author nor I meet that criterion. However, in light of its title and theme, that is probably as it should be—backward and upside down from the way things are usually done.

I first met Jordan after listening to him speak to a room full of teenagers at a summer camp near McCall, Idaho. I was intrigued by his approach to those adolescents. Rather than cracking jokes and entertaining them with stories, he simply delivered an unembellished gospel message, challenging those teens to engage Jesus Christ as Lord. And to my surprise, he connected, and many of them responded!

Sensing something unique about this young man and curious to know his story, I later sought him out in the dining hall. Following several hours of conversation, he asked if I would be willing to spend regular time with him as a spiritual mentor. That was my next clue that this twenty-six-year-old was not cut from the same cloth as most young men his age are. Even though he had already successfully built a ministry to over two hundred young adults and was promised greater things ahead (as you'll read in this book), he wanted to open his life to this seventy-two-year-old retired pastor!

That was a year and a half ago, and I can say unequivocally that our monthly meetings have become highlights in this season of my life. Jordan frequently expresses gratitude for my listening ear and wise counsel, and I receive his gratitude as sincere. But I must say that I am humbled by it because I continually learn so much from him.

As you read Jordan's story, I expect you're likely to wonder, as I do, how someone as young as Jordan can speak with such wisdom and demonstrate such life-impacting power as he does. It is that very question that he addresses in the pages that follow.

The apostle Paul captured the essence of this story when he wrote to the Corinthian church, "We carry this precious Message around in the unadorned clay pots of our ordinary lives. That's to prevent anyone from confusing God's incomparable power with us" (2 Corinthians 4:7 *The Message)*. This book is about the "unadorned clay pot" of a man named Jordan Verner. As you read it, I hope you'll catch the heart of his message: that it is only through our brokenness that the light of "God's incomparable power" has a chance to shine out into the darkness.

Jordan's story is, in truth, unique to him alone, but at the same time, its core principles are applicable to every one of us. Few of us have mothers who intercede with the passion and persistence that his mother does. But every one of us knows what it means to be humbled by our inability to become all we are created to be.

My prayer is that you will be encouraged through spending time walking with Jordan through the ups and downs of his passionate life. And when all is said and done, hopefully you will be strengthened in your resolve to follow Jesus through the valleys of your own pain and into the heights He holds before you.

ACKNOWLEDGMENTS

THERE ARE A NUMBER OF INDIVIDUALS I WANT TO HONOR FOR YOUR involvement in the creative process of this work. First, thank you Rick and Amie for your patience, perspective, and diligence in creating this alongside me.

Rick, your probing questions compelled me to dig deeper than I would have myself in searching for language and words to express the inspiration I felt within my heart. The refinement process you incited cleared away much dirt and debris from the simple truths Jesus desired to reveal in this work. Thank you for your investment; your fingerprints have marked this greatly!

Amie, thank you for saying yes to embarking on this unknown journey and for the excellence you brought to the table. There were so many times where you worked your magic and brought precision where my words had wandered. It was so much fun learning the art of creative writing from the many, many mistakes you kindly identified. You taught me so much. It was a blessing having you on this team!

Susanna, thank you for the words of encouragement along the way, as well as the many commas you added and deleted. I never knew how little I understood the minutiae of English grammar until seeing your marks on the pages!

To the leadership team of River House church, thank you for encouraging and championing me to step out and actually do this.

Authoring a book was something I knew I would someday do, but that "someday" was far away in my mind. The Lord used you profoundly to bring this to the forefront of my heart and catalyze the creation process. I love you all so much.

Lastly, to the whole River House family, thank you for all the prayer, honor, and love you have shown me these last two years. My big prayer in writing this is that it will add fuel to the fire of what is already burning in our midst. It is an honor to run with you all and weekly be inspired by what God is doing through us as a community. We are demonstrating the power of a nameless, faceless revival, and I am so privileged to be a part of it. Thank you for allowing me the privilege of speaking into your lives, all the while growing as a communicator of God's word. I am forever marked by the beauty of this family.

PREFACE

IT WAS A TUESDAY EVENING IN MAY WHEN THE LORD PUT THE unction in me to write this book. It came through the encouragement of the leadership team of the church I pastor. A wise woman looked at me and told me that I needed to write and renew people's minds about what it means to build the church. I knew she was hearing from God because this statement aligned with what I had prayed privately earlier that morning. As I reflected on this, two things came to mind. The first was that starting a church is no different from accomplishing anything else God has called us to create. In that sense, this book will have universal application to anyone desiring to enter into a dynamic place of partnering with God. The second was that the core of this book would be about humility. It would be a great disservice to glamorize this process and write only of ministry success and miracle testimonies without prefacing that these triumphs were birthed from a place of great brokenness.

The gospel's core message is that we must die to live. Many Christians wonder why they do not abide in resurrection power. The answer is quite simple: they haven't yet died. I struggle using so strong a word as *death* in the preface because I don't want you to put the book down! Yet I assure you that the reward is worth the cost. The kingdom of God is an upside down kingdom, and the path of humility is one that leads to the high place of co-creating with God through the Holy Spirit.

Proverbs 29:18 states, "Where there is no prophetic vision, the people cast off restraint." The Body of Christ is lacking prophetic vision regarding the pursuit of humility. Humility is a pearl of great price that we must seek to understand and search for like fine treasure. Years ago, the Lord spoke to me out of Ezekiel 16 and told me that if I wanted to know humility, I needed to study these verses. In this passage of scripture, God walks by a baby girl (Israel) writhing in her own blood (shame). He saves her, proceeds to crown her with the finest clothing and jewels, and makes her an object of praise in the earth. Humility is knowing exactly who you are without Christ (writhing in your own sin and shame) and exactly who you are in Christ (a royal son or daughter) at the same time! Like Paul, we must carry both the death and the resurrection power of Jesus with us each day (2 Corinthians 4:10–11).

In the pages that follow, I will disclose the process God took me through of learning to die and bridge this to the fruitful consequences of abiding with God. My hope is that you will be filled with clarity regarding the intentionality of God's work in your life as you read. God is endlessly creative in how He deals with us, so I will present to you not a formula, but a story. Stories are artifacts that help us find meaning and make sense of our lives. I will use the term *artifacts,* defined simply as things that we as human beings create, throughout this work. From the beginning of history, humanity has been at work creating stories. We use stories to interpret our circumstances. This applies to the big questions of life, such as "Why are we here?" and "Where did we come from?" Yet it also applies to our simple daily routines.

An illustration of this would be a teenage driver who hits a tree with his car (for the sake of this example, he is perfectly fine, but the car is totaled). One of his friends, named Johnnie, drives by and sees his buddy talking with the police on the side of the road. He whispers to himself, "What an idiot!" while he continues by without another thought. This story—"What an idiot!"—is what Johnnie used to interpret the event. He has no idea of the details of what happened, but Johnnie tells himself, "What an idiot!" because that helps him interpret the event in a way that makes him feel safe. If his friend is an idiot, that makes Johnnie feel more secure about his own well-being driving the car. It distances Johnnie from experiencing the vulnerable truth—that the same thing could happen to him! A few minutes later, Johnnie's mom drives by the same scene, but the story she tells herself is, "That could have been my son!" She is immediately flooded with panic and picks up her phone and dials Johnnie to make sure he is wearing his seatbelt. In this example, the same event is interpreted in two completely different ways that evoke two very different responses. This is one very small example that demonstrates the power of the stories we tell. Stories influence the emotional responses we have in the circumstances we face. They can be used to evoke fear, doubt, and confusion. They can also be used to create joy and serenity. My greatest prayer in sharing my story is that it be a kingdom artifact that God whispers through—bringing hope, healing, courage, and freedom.

This is not just my story. It belongs to another just as much as it does me. It is no longer I who live, but Christ who lives in me. We are walking this life together, and so in the same way, we write this book together. I cannot stress the importance of this enough. My goal is not to inspire you with what I believe to be the right way to interpret life. My intent is to reveal the goodness of Jesus through my life in hopes that He will become your story, just as He has become mine. His perspective is full of wisdom and exudes incontrovertible hope. We need this to fulfill our purpose on earth. Buckle up—we're going for a ride!

INTRODUCTION

In the beginning God created the Heavens and the
Earth. The earth was formless and void, and darkness
was over the surface of the deep, and the Spirit of
God was moving over the surface of the waters.

GENESIS 1:1–2

T HE FIRST KNOWN ACT OF GOD RECORDED IN SCRIPTURE WAS THE
creation of the cosmos. Out of nothing, God created the earth and
all that is in it. Our God is a creative genius. It is in the context of this
narrative that we learn that we are created in the image of the Creator
(Genesis 1:26). Humankind is not an eternally existent race but was
birthed through the creative force of God. God imagined us, *seeing*
us, though we were still unformed, and then fashioned us according
to what He saw. Perhaps the most dynamic gift God bestowed upon
the human race was the imagination. He first used this gift when
forming the world, and then in His goodness, He graced humanity
with its power. The ability to imagine is what has empowered every
invention known to man. I marvel at the reality that God put human
beings on a raw, uncultivated planet and somehow we have figured
out how to use Earth's resources to fashion metal machines that fly

faster than the speed of sound! We are an endlessly creative race because we are formed in the image of an endlessly creative God.

Very simply put, the highest call of God upon His image-bearers is to co-*create* kingdom artifacts that demonstrate the fulfillment of the Lord's prayer: "Thy kingdom come and Thy will be done on Earth as it is in heaven." God created humankind and put us in a garden, but we read in Revelation that the destination we are sojourning toward is a city, the heavenly Jerusalem. This is amazing because a city is a hub of human culture! Ken Myers defines culture as "what human beings make of the world—in both senses."[1] In other words, it is the physical creations we *make* and how we *make sense of* what they mean. An example of this would be a business. This is a physical creation that most often consists of an office, a product, a staff, and a business plan. A business has many physical, material dimensions to it, but it also has deep meaning woven into as well. Perhaps the owner has a passion for the poor and so seeks to employ many underprivileged people into the organization. Perhaps then a culture is being created where the rich and the poor exist in the same workplace learning from and working alongside one another. This is highly valuable but very difficult to quantify or calculate. This is a microcosm of culture. It is both the material creations we produce and the immaterial, and sometimes intangible, meanings that are attached to the creations.

God began the creation process when He spoke "Let there be light," but He did not complete it. He placed us in a garden and then gave us authority to co-create our world hand in hand with Him. He is a Father who delights in empowering His children to do great things. He has plans and dreams for our lives. He wants us to build on top of the foundation He has laid. He has purpose assigned to our lives, and it is fulfilled in the mandate to create! We have been given the creative faculty of the imagination in order to create artifacts that literally change the world. However, our highest call is not fulfilled in simply creating good things—good things can be created by anyone; we are made to create "God things." These are divine-human creations birthed from communion with God Himself.

This word, *communion,* is defined as the sharing or exchanging of intimate thoughts and feelings. God jealousy desires this type of intimate connection with each one of us (James 5:4). In the mystery of communion with God, something happens within a man or woman that unlocks supernatural power. Creature and Creator become united in a bond that results in a creative explosion of kingdom fruitfulness (John 15). "God things" are created that begin to transform the world. We begin living in such a way that people observe us and are left saying, "Only God! Only God could do that, or create that, or know that!" There is literally no end to what this can look like! The world is desperately in need of families, books, media, businesses, governmental strategies, educational models, and churches that leave people exclaiming, "Only God!" God is the creative genius of the ages, and He has uniquely designed you in such a way that the partnership of your life with His will result in the most incredible kingdom artifacts the world could imagine.

The truth is that we were born to create these artifacts out of the place of intimate communion with Jesus. When we do this, we are bringing His world into ours. God has a way of doing business, a way of governing, a way of parenting, a way of teaching, a way of doing everything—and the world is longing to see what that is! God is a genius, and so everything He does works really, really well! He is the answer to every problem known to man, and we have access to these answers only in the place of communion.

The big hiccup in all of this is sin. The fall of humankind corrupted this design and alienated humanity from God. We rebelled and chose this. In the vacuum that resulted, the mandate to create the kingdom of God on earth was forfeited and our original design forgotten. In His great love, God sent Jesus to purchase the redemption of humanity in His blood. This redemption is comprehensive. Jesus did not just come to save us from sin, but He also came to reinstate the kingdom mandate and make a way for humankind to once again fulfill our destiny on earth. The cross is central to all of this. That is why a book on creativity must be linked to humility. The greatest act of humility ever demonstrated was the surrender of Jesus Christ to the cross of Calvary. His death is what opened the door for humanity to enter back into communion with the Father and receive hope once again of fulfilling our creative purpose on earth.

This is the mandate and destiny of every human being. This is not a theory to me but something that's becoming my reality. What is to follow is not a how-to on doing amazing things with God but a depiction of painful, costly lessons that prepared the way for God to bear profound fruit through my life. I pray to God that this creation you have in your hands will awaken things dormant within you and be an instrument through which His creative force flows mightily. The world is waiting for what you have to give.

PART ONE

"There Is a Time to Tear Down"

Ecclesiastes 3:3

CHAPTER ONE

Two Encounters

The Spirit of the Lord is upon me ... He has sent
me to proclaim liberty to the captives.

———

LUKE 4:18

I WAS RAISED IN A CONSERVATIVE CHRISTIAN HOME AND HAVE memories of being at church throughout my entire life. My mother was a closet charismatic in a conservative denomination that was not open to the gifts of the Holy Spirit. I paid no attention to this dichotomy at the time, yet I was keenly aware that morning devotions with Mom possessed something powerful that I never experienced at church. The truth is that I found church so boring that I absolutely dreaded going! Due to my mother's devotional leadership and exemplary life of prayer, I was discipled to love the presence of God at a young age. This instilled a deep faith within me. I knew God was real, and I never questioned whether or not I wanted to live my life for Him.

This discrepancy I saw between my mother's passionate love for Jesus and the sterile, boring nature of church life gave me a confused notion about God's activity in our lives. Though I had no language for this growing up, I caught the idea that God was to be experienced powerfully in your private life, but making your public life fulfilling was up to you. In this confusion, I turned to athletics as a means to find purpose and joy. I began forging an identity based on my success and notoriety as an athlete. As I progressed into my teenage years, I found myself battling feelings of increasing emptiness, no matter how much success I achieved in the public arena. I never turned my back on God through these years, though I was keenly aware that He was secondary to my athletic success. This was not a conscious decision I was making, but rather the result of going to church week after week my whole life and finding it completely irrelevant and powerless. This repeated, habitual experience preached a message much louder than any sermon I had ever heard. It convinced me that God was not working powerfully in real life but only in devotional time.

I grew emptier and emptier as time passed, and I eventually began medicating my pain with various "pet" sins. I was convinced I could control these little habits and tried my best to justify my actions. My go-to justifier was comparing myself to others who were doing far worse things. I kept all my sins hidden from the public eye, and in every way I looked the part of a perfect Christian boy. I was a good student, didn't party, wasn't sleeping around with girls, and was a stellar athlete. I had been affirmed so many times in this that I was convinced I was doing everything perfectly.

Looking back, it's easy to see how much pain I was in, but at the time, I was so ignorant. I was perishing in my blindness, and it was here that God stepped in and began a deep work of grace. I thank God that He loves us so much that He refuses to let us remain in mediocrity. He died and rose so we could live in the fullness of Christ.

Everyone thought I looked like a perfect kid, but this excluded those who knew me best—my family. I had unleashed my pain upon my younger brother for years in the form of verbal abuse. Hurting people hurt people, and the wounds evident in our relationship demonstrate how much pain I was truly in. My mother had been watching this unfold in my life for a number of years, and she was grieved by the pride she saw rising up in me. She began interceding for me, asking that God would set me free, and I can undoubtedly confess that her prayers are what saved my life. I was arrogant, with a sharp mind and a shut heart, and no person was capable of penetrating the walls I had built up. But what is impossible for people is possible for God.

I was seventeen years old and a junior in high school when the Lord stepped in and revealed His power to me in two very distinct ways. I will do my best to describe each encounter in a way that captures the impact they had upon me.

It was late in the evening, and I was in the kitchen of my family's home. My mother and I were discussing something I can't remember (though I do recall not having the best attitude about it). At one point in the conversation, she looked at me with astonishment and nearly yelled, "You need to sit down right now and tell me the lie you are believing!" It is worthwhile to mention that this was an uncommon thing for her to say. This statement struck me as being out of left field. I was so stunned that all I could do was laugh. Again she said, "Sit down and tell me the lie you are believing!" The second time, I got offended and began to storm off. (That was a bad idea!) She almost roared at me to sit my behind on the kitchen chair, and I obeyed. She then began praying out loud, and I became extremely irritated. At this point, my father walked into the kitchen and asked what was happening. My mom explained, "He is believing a lie, and he's not leaving until he tells me what it is." To my utter disbelief, my dad was on board and joined her at the table! I don't say this to knock on my father, but when I was growing up, he was never the spiritual one. Outside of this memory, I cannot recall a time where my dad was a part of any kind of spiritual experience. Yet in this instance, he was not only on board, but he supported my mother wholeheartedly and would not let me leave the table.

I was sitting at the table, so angry I could explode, with my mom praying loudly and my father staring at me. This may have been the weirdest experience of my childhood! My mom was determined and continued demanding, "Tell me the lie you are believing!" over and over again. A long time passed in this standoff—at least ten or fifteen minutes. Eventually, my anger began to subside, and I began to see a thought form in my head. I don't know how to describe the sensation, but it started as a whisper and then grew louder and louder. Eventually, it grew so loud within my head that it felt as though someone was screaming. I knew this was the lie my mother was demanding me to confess. I tried to speak it, but my mouth would not move. Tears began to flow down my face, and snot began dripping down my nose, but still I could not speak. At this point, my mom was practically screaming in her prayer language, and while I still to this day find that a little weird, it ultimately worked! At last, I opened my mouth and spoke the lie that I later realized I had rehearsed to myself a thousand times: "I don't need anyone but God."

When those words left my tongue, it was as if five hundred pounds lifted off my body, and I felt peace for the first time in a very long time. I had absolutely no idea what had happened to me, but I felt freedom! I now know that what I experienced was deliverance from a demonic stronghold of pride. This was my first breakthrough in this area of my life. In pastoral ministry, I have seen some confusion over the nature of what a breakthrough is. Many wrongly believe that these powerful moments of liberation are the end of the battle. I have found this to be quite the opposite.

Using a military analogy, a breakthrough in battle is when you penetrate an enemy's stronghold or defense. It is great a moment of victory! But a breakthrough must be quickly followed through if that momentary victory is to be established and the enemy taken. It is no different in the spiritual sense. This experience with my mom was when my eyes were first opened to the battle I was in.

I learned through this encounter that lies only have power over us when they are kept in silence. When we speak them out, their influence is diminished. I immediately recognized that those words were the fruit of self-protective pride. I rehearsed them any time I was hurting or feeling rejected so I could receive a twisted form of self-comfort. I would convince myself that I was going to become someone great so I could prove to the world how special I was. Once I spoke these words out loud, I recognized that I had been deceived. Jesus refers to Satan as the father of lies, and so he is. He is the great deceiver, and when we partner with what he says to us, it leads to destructive behavior that closes us off from the presence of God. Being seventeen, I lacked the wisdom to fully process the implications of this event until much later, but it was significant nonetheless. I found a fresh vibrancy in my relationship with God and a greater understanding of His power at work in my life.

This event helped open the eyes and ears of my heart so that I would be ready to hear what the Lord wanted to say to me. The lies of hell blind our eyes and deafen our ears to what God is speaking— similar to a radio dial that is out of tune, the static gets so loud that we can't hear the music. That was me before the kitchen-table deliverance. In my heart, I loved Jesus, but the lie I was believing had opened me to so much static that I was deaf to His voice.

Seven months later, God met me again. It was a rough week, and I was really hurting. We often judge pain as bad because it's not fun. Pain is energy, however, and we can channel it into a very raw form of praise that opens our hearts to the comfort of the Holy Spirit. Look no further than the Psalms for examples of what this looks like. I was alone in my bedroom, processing my pain before the Lord, and in the middle of this, He showed up! I didn't have words for it at the time, but I began to have a vision. This was remarkable for me because I was unaware that people had visions and was in no way seeking one. All I knew was I *saw* something.

What I saw was a path, and I intuitively knew that it was the path of my life—and it was horrifying. It was pure selfishness, and I was convicted to the core. In that moment, the façade of being the perfect Christian boy was dashed to pieces, and I knew I was on a path that completely revolved around myself. I was terrified. I began to scream, "God, don't let me go down that path! I surrender my life to You! I'll do it Your way. Just don't let me go down that path!" What came out of my mouth was so raw that I remember thinking with each word, "What are you praying? This is going to ruin your life!" This was unlike any prayer I had ever prayed. I knew with unwavering faith that God was going to answer that cry, and that made me very nervous.

As I journeyed on from that day, passion for Jesus began oozing out of me in ways that made me uncomfortable. I was having a hard time accepting what was happening inside of me. I liked it but felt awkward at the same time. Similar to when teenagers grow so quickly that they lose their coordination—that was me in the spiritual realm. God accomplished something very deep in me during my seventeenth year, and it was all orchestrated according to His timing. A mighty storm was brewing on the horizon of my life, and He was depositing in me what was necessary to endure it.

CHAPTER TWO

Deep Sadness

Unless a grain of wheat falls into the ground and dies
it remains alone, but if it dies it will bear much fruit.

————

JOHN 12:24

W<small>E ARE PROMISED SUFFERING IN THIS LIFE</small> (2 T<small>IMOTHY</small> 3:12) <small>AND</small>
are told to embrace it, allowing the process to fashion saints of
us (James 1:2-4). A term often used to describe this is "carrying your
cross." Jesus clearly tells us, "Whoever does not carry his cross and
follow Me cannot be My disciple" (Luke 14:27). Jesus, of course, is
not referring to the physical act of carrying a Roman, wooden cross
and being publicly murdered. That was *His* cross. He is telling us we

must carry *our* cross. A. W. Tozer quotes an unknown saint in his work *The Radical Cross* and writes:

> God is ingenious in making us crosses. He may make them of iron and of lead which are heavy of themselves. He makes some of straw which seem to weigh nothing, but one discovers they are no less difficult to carry. A cross that appears of straw so that others think it amounts to nothing may be crucifying you through and through.
>
> He makes some with gold and precious stones which dazzle the spectators and excite the envy of the public but which crucify no less than the crosses which are more despised.[2]

As Christians we get into trouble when we compare our sufferings. Ultimately, pain is pain and everyone will have to face it. God has a cross with your name on it because He is good and He loves you. We do not get to choose our crosses; they will choose us. Our job is to embrace this gift of severe mercy and let it accomplish its purpose in our lives.

Undeniably, there is only one purpose of a cross, and that is the complete destruction of the one it is assigned to. Your cross is given to kill you and put your selfish nature in the grave. Carrying our crosses is not a one-time event, or even a season of our Christian walk, but a lifelong journey of being a disciple. The truth is that no matter how sanctified we have become, there is always a deeper work of grace to be accomplished.

However, in the journey of carrying your cross, there is an intensified experience of spiritual death, usually (but not always) taking place later in the Christian's journey, referred to throughout Christian history as "the dark night of the soul." This is a moment of time when God removes all feeling of His presence. In this time, despair invades our souls, and we are left alone with only our faith to stand on.[3]

Jesus lived a life of suffering (Isaiah 53:3), but His dark night occurred while hanging on the cross. He cried out in despair, "Father, why have you forsaken Me?" and yet still entrusted Himself in faith to His God. Following Jesus, our example, we too must go through the crucible of the dark night of the soul if we are to become who we were born to be. Jesus did not come and die so we would not have to. He went to the cross and was broken by the very worst of human severity so that our dark night of the soul would not be the end of the story. He rose, and so in faith we know that we will too.

Each story of brokenness is both universal and highly unique. Regardless of how universal suffering is to the human race, it remains a very difficult thing to relate to. When you are dying, you die alone (John 12:24). I imagine that though John and Mary were only a few feet from Jesus's body as He hung, they were endless oceans from the pain of His great heart. Tozer captured this best when he wrote, "There are some things too sacred for any eye to look upon but God's."[4] In light of this, I want to make clear that the goal of sharing my story with you is not to make you understand my pain. That is a fruitless endeavor. Rather, I will only highlight my sufferings and focus on the universally relatable aspects of my story in an attempt to bring solidarity to your own. The path of suffering has a tendency of feeling like a random wandering through a barren land, when in truth it is an ancient road that's been traveled by saints for centuries. My hope is that you find comfort as you read, knowing you are with God on this sacred pilgrimage.

In May of 2008, I crossed into a dark night and what felt like an abyss of great suffering. My cross came and found me, and though I wanted to, I could not escape it. For the next three and a half years, I carried my cross and died alone. I'm not going to attempt to capture every detail of this, but I will only highlight both the external and internal nature of the pain. I share this to create a context for what is to come. The importance is not so much the details of the suffering but the greatness of His redemption.

My process was triggered by the collapse of my family. I witnessed a horrible trauma of betrayal that scourged my soul with fear. I watched people I love weep like wounded animals as addiction broke into my home like an armed man, stealing everything. I had a front-row seat to witness divorce kill the covenant that brought me into this life. The foundation of my identity was shaken, and I was made vulnerable to addiction and torment that made me feel like someone was holding my head underwater. I felt as though I were suffocating, and I couldn't catch my breath no matter how hard I tried. My heart was broken by one who was my protector, and my soul was crushed. I wept for so many days that at one point I couldn't consciously remember one without tears. Despair possessed me, and depression clouded my whole being with a fog. I could not see God, nor feel God, nor hear God. At that point, the darkness I was experiencing was far more powerful than anything I had ever known, including my personal experience with Jesus. I learned in these days that spiritual warfare is a real phenomenon. There is an adversary who prowls like a roaring lion seeking to steal, kill, and destroy (John 10:10). I was ignorant of what was happening, and this only amplified my suffering.

During this season, I began hearing voices that haunted me. It was so intense at times that I couldn't pray because the thoughts flooding my mind were so loud and disgusting. I now know that this was spiritual attack and the voices belonged to the demonic realm, but at the time, I thought that I was going crazy. When my mind began to be flooded with dark thoughts, I had no idea how to process them, so I would enter into a state of survival where I tried my best to numb my mind in order to silence the torment. I was terrified that I would be put into an institution if I told anyone, and so I kept my mouth shut.

My confusion in this situation stemmed from the fact that I was raised in an environment in which it was never affirmed that I was able to hear from God. Because of this, I had a certain skepticism associated with hearing His voice. Years later, God's grace liberated me from this misconception when the voice of my Father found me.

Once I realized I could hear His voice, it was easy to recognize I need not pay attention to any other. Yet this realization did not come immediately, and I remained for a long time in a state of internal crisis that in many ways outweighed the external traumas I was experiencing. I truly thought I had lost my mind and I would never live a normal day again. I was living in an internal chaos that I could not escape.

This suffering produced something very good in me that I'm convinced would have come about no other way. Pain has an invigorating effect on the human body. It is similar to when you jump into ice cold water—no matter what you felt before, you suddenly are wide awake. This was my experience when the pain crashed in. I found myself powerfully alert and highly motivated to find a way out of suffering. There are only two ways to accomplish this: one is self-medication, and the other is the healing love of Jesus. Self-medication will take your pain away temporarily but increase it over time. It takes away feeling but allows the wound to fester and the infection to spread; there is no true healing involved in this. The only thing that will ever bring healing to a human heart is the love of Jesus.

As I wrote before, I had fully surrendered to Jesus only one year prior to this chaos breaking loose around me. This left me in a big predicament as to how to handle my pain. I was faced with deciding between my way or God's way, which intimidated me because I knew His way meant no instant relief. I will confess openly to you that I self-medicated my pain away for the first four months. I quickly realized this failed to provide any real comfort and, by the grace of God, was saved from losing myself in sexual addiction. He told me I needed to suffer well, which meant no more self-medication. I was to find my comfort in Him.

What followed was a very messy process trying to make sense of the chaos I was experiencing—both externally and internally. I was searching desperately for truth that could set me free from the deep anguish I was drowning in. What follows is a depiction of some of the treasures I found while digging in the dirt of my brokenness.

The biggest temptation I faced during this time of calamity was to put God on trial and begin challenging His goodness. Falling into this trap is destructive, as it creates susceptibility to self-justifying thought patterns that push us deeper and deeper into self-medication. I would be lying if I said I never questioned God during this season, because I did. I wanted to know why "Mighty to Save" didn't seem to be rescuing me. I wanted to know why the depression that was devouring my strength and emotions wouldn't go away. I wanted to know why the people I was turning to for comfort were rejecting me. I wanted to know why divorce came to my family. I wanted to know why He wouldn't make the voices stop. I was scared and confused, and I wanted answers desperately.

I've learned that God is able to handle our questions, and if we keep walking with Him with an open heart, He will be faithful to bring goodness to bear. Where we get in trouble is when we grow bitter, close off our hearts, and act as if God is required to prove who He is to us. This behavior belies spiritual immaturity. It is no different from when a toddler, when denied something he or she wants, throws a fit—the toddler does not recognize the parent is operating out of love, but instead is fixated on what he or she thinks is best. I am not trying to be insensitive here, for I know many people have gone through horrible trauma and heartache. At the same time, we must understand that no matter how much suffering we have experienced, Jesus had it worse. He was tortured with a wrath and cruelty no human being deserves, much less the Creator and King. Jesus was victimized, but He was never a victim. He never wallowed in self-pity. He did not allow Himself to question the Father or close off His heart but instead faithfully entrusted Himself to God, humbling himself in dependence even to the point of death (Philippians 2:8). If we confess to be disciples of Jesus, ones set apart to follow and be like the Master, then we must be prepared to suffer in the same manner as our Lord (Galatians 2:20, Romans 8:17–18).

By far my biggest point of contention in doing this was trying to wrap my head around the relationship between God's goodness and human suffering. At the time, I had no grid to distinguish that God using pain did not equate to Him authoring it. This left me to wonder if I could really trust God. I intuitively began asking myself, "If these horrible things are taking place, could God still be good?" As I wrestled with this over multiple years, I eventually came to realize that though God allows suffering, He does not cause it. This meaning that God did not will my parents' divorce, even though He allowed it. And that though God allowed the torment I was experiencing, He didn't conceive of or desire it.

This sounds like a minor clarification, but I must emphasize it is not. This revelation liberated me to interpret my sufferings in a way that maintained the absolute goodness of God in the midst of it. This enabled me to walk through suffering with the comfort of knowing God was with me, and not punishing me. Let me explain.

Witnessing the destruction of my family was a brutal experience, something no one wants to go through. In the years that followed, there was always the hope that God would work a miracle and restore what had been stolen. In my case, this did not happen as my mother, my brothers, and many others had hoped and prayed. This added sorrow to sorrow. In times of disappointment, the sentiment is often expressed, "It just must not have been God's will." Frankly, these words disturb me. I have never allowed myself to speak those words in regard to what happened, and didn't happen, in my parents' marriage.

In the wake of my father's remarriage, and consequently the final seal that my nuclear family would never be restored, the first thing I did after their ceremony was withdraw to a secluded dock on a lake to be with the Lord. My heart was overburdened with grief, heartache, and disappointment, but nevertheless, I began to lift up my heart in worship. The words that flowed from my lips were these: "My God, you are a covenant-maker and a covenant-keeper, and I worship you! I didn't get to see this miracle. I didn't get to see Your will be done in my family, and it is so painful. But please use me as an instrument to reverse the curse of divorce in this world so others will never have to experience the pain I'm feeling today!" This was one of the most powerful moments I have ever had with the Lord. I sensed His presence tangibly with me. I was in so much pain, but He was there.

The reason I could pray this prayer and worship God in the midst of a great disappointment was because I had come into the understanding that God is good even in the midst of suffering. Knowing that God was suffering alongside me comforted my heart. It assured me that I could trust Him. He is not a removed deity coldly observing the affairs of man (John 11:35). He is intimately involved and actively working with His people to bring good to the earth. He doesn't will divorce, murder, and all the heinous things that take place on this planet, but He does allow them.

Why? Because God is a God of love, and love only exists where there is freedom. Even in Eden, the garden of perfection, there was choice. God allowed the tree of good and evil to grow in the middle of the garden, meaning that a terrible choice was made available in a perfect place. If humans have no choice, then love cannot exist. I doubt there is a woman on earth who dreams of a man proposing to her because he *has* to. What makes marriage so special is that two people enter into a covenant because they *want* to. In a similar way, God desires that we use the freedom we've been given to choose Him. Unfortunately, many are blinded by the prince of the air (Ephesians 2:2) and have gone after other gods.

The good news is that God works all things to the good of those who love Him (Romans 8:28). This means God wastes nothing! If He allows suffering and trials, He will surely use them to create goodness and beauty that will take your breath away and leave you in a puddle of joyful tears (Psalm 126). I can testify to this truth. I have witnessed Him turning ashes into beauty time and time again. Very rarely has any of this looked like what I would have thought, but He has continually proven that no matter the amount of destruction, He can and will turn it for good.

I don't claim to have a complete answer to the question, "Why does God allow bad things to take place?" but I do know that human actions must be accounted for. Humans are powerful beings and have chosen to use their freedom to make selfish decisions that have resulted in generations of suffering. God allows this because He isn't controlling humanity, but has chosen to save the world through relationships built on love. He values love too much to step in and control people. It would be a violation of His very essence. What this means is that instead of getting offended with God in our pain, we are able to choose to entrust ourselves to His Spirit like Jesus did (Luke 23:46) and allow Him to turn our crosses of suffering into symbols of hope for a world craving it. This is what God empowered me to do that day on the dock, and He will do the same for you.

To do this, we must turn from focusing on the suffering itself and shift to what I call a "remnant perspective." This term refers to a perspective gleaned from looking at the story of Israel retrospectively. When viewing the biblical narrative in hindsight, you can see all throughout the history of Israel that God was always preserving a righteous remnant for Himself. Even in times of the greatest suffering, this remnant remained. This perspective has helped me discover the redemption and goodness of God woven all throughout scripture, as well as my own life.

In stories such as Noah and the flood, we tend to focus on the flood and the destruction of the wicked. This causes us to begin asking questions that have no concrete answers, such as "Why did all those people die?" and, "Did God really love the world?" These questions are similar to the questions I would ask God concerning my own sufferings. These reveal I was more focused on my pain than I was on Him. To understand God more fully in the scriptures, and in our own stories, we must find the remnant of His working. In the case of the flood, the remnant is Noah. We must begin asking new questions, such as "Why did God preserve Noah and speak to him about the things to come?" and "Why did God constantly preserve a people for Himself, no matter how much they rebelled and turned their backs on Him?" Questions like this help us recognize that even in the midst of calamity and what seems like chaos breaking loose on earth, God's intentions are good and His salvation is at work. The reality is that sometimes we only come to see this retrospectively.

As humans, we are prone to giving so much attention and energy to the negativity in life that we fail to recognize the activity of God. Colossians 3:2 tells us to "set your mind on the things above, and not on the things that are on earth. For you have died, and your life is now hidden with Christ in God." Setting our minds on the things above is not scriptural grounds to deny reality and live in the clouds, but a discipline of learning to fix our eyes upon Jesus in and above all the circumstances we face. Especially in trials, when the wind and the waves are raging all around us, it is even more imperative that we have developed the capacity to lock our gaze upon King Jesus.

The life of King David reveals what this looks like in practical terms. When he was a young boy, he was prophesized to be be the king of Israel, and after that point, he lived a life marked by conflict and rejection. He experienced betrayal from his own family, his king whom he loyally served, and lastly, the people of Israel. This forced him to flee to the Philistine lands and take refuge in a city called Ziklag. During the years of fleeing from Saul as a political exile, he amassed a following of societal outcasts. These outcasts would eventually come to be known as "David's Mighty Men," implying the effect of David's leadership upon these misfits. The climax of David's troubles came on a day when he arrived home to Ziklag to find their city burned and the women and children taken captive. It was in this moment of crisis that his own "Mighty Men" turned on him and contemplated stoning David!

Needless to say, in that moment there was plenty of negativity that he could have focused on! I can only imagine that he was tempted to put God on trial. However, in this low place, David did not express anger or give into despair but instead withdrew and strengthened himself in the Lord his God (1 Samuel 30:6). David was seeking to stay "in tune" with what God was doing rather than despairing over what He wasn't. It is recorded that in this dire time, with a foreign army carrying his people away and his men ready to kill him, David asked God, "Shall I pursue this band? Shall I overtake them?" (1 Samuel 30:8). Crisis reveals character, and therefore this story demonstrates that even in pain, disappointment, and rejection, David's heart was radically yielded to the will of God. He had trained himself through habitual experience to put his focus upon the Lord. God told him to go and reclaim the women and children, which he did. That very evening, he discovered that Saul had died and he was now the king of Israel. The promise was at last fulfilled. God's ways are not our ways, but He is always working for our good.

We must recognize that when we put God on trial we are closing ourselves off from His grace and resisting His purposes. Even when it makes no sense, the person who is after the heart of God will entrust himself or herself fully to Him, just like Jesus and King David did. This posture allows His grace to flow unhindered through us, turning our cries of agony into shouts of resounding joy.

In my own story, a decade has now passed. The perspective I hold now gives me the luxury of better comprehending where God was through those dark days. Though I was not aware of it at the time, I can now clearly recognize the remnant of God's working in me. There are a few experiences that together capture how the grace of God was operating on my behalf.

A few months after everything hit the fan, my mother was awakened at night from a dream. God speaking through dreams was not something we were familiar with, as we were in an environment that never spoke of such phenomena. In the dream, God showed my mom a vision of me walking through a season of suffering and darkness and, at the end of the dream, an image of His glory surrounding me. When my mother communicated to me what she had seen, I got emotional and sick to my stomach—emotional because I knew it was God and sick because of the word *suffering*. I had never before considered suffering with Jesus. I thought surrender meant He would bring fulfillment. It was no more than a couple of weeks later that the voices began haunting my mind. As I plummeted into darkness, my hope came to rest solely on the validity of this dream. In a deep place within, I clung to His promise that His glory would surround me, whatever that might look like.

A number of months later, my mother again came to me having heard from God on my behalf, yet this time it was through a passage of scripture. She came to me and read this verse: "Peter, Peter, Satan has demanded to sift you like wheat, but do not fear, I have prayed for you" (Luke 22:31). Though this is a "scary" verse, it ministered to me in these days of trial because it reassured me that I was not alone in my suffering. It helped define what was happening—I was being sifted so that impurities within me would be removed.

This knowledge helped open my eyes to the reality that I had something to learn in this process. The truth was, I was broken. This seemed like a shameful thing to admit at the time, but now I laugh about that. I'm more aware of my brokenness now than I was then, and there's no more shame attached. Brokenness is a beautiful thing when you allow Jesus to permeate it. Anyway, I realized that the darkness I was walking through in some measure was linked to impurity within my heart. I didn't have to look far to recognize the brokenness and sin that I housed within. I became voraciously hungry for truth and was willing to look at my brokenness for the first time in my life. This was because I wanted out of pain.

For the first time in my life, I opened myself to receiving help. I began periodically seeking out professional counseling. After listening to me process about my circumstances in a session one day, my counselor made a statement that I will never forget: "It seems like God is wanting you to learn humility." His words stung me, and I did my best to act as if I were not offended. This was because they made me admit for the first time that there was pride in me that needed to be dealt with. I didn't like the thought of this, but something deep within knew it was true. In the aftermath, I began pondering what pride was and how to get rid of it. My motivation was to alleviate the pain I was experiencing. I reasoned that if I got rid of pride, I wouldn't need to be sifted any longer and God could bring me into His blessing.

Looking back, I was like a blind squirrel looking for a nut called humility. I had no idea what it meant, but something within me became fascinated with the pursuit. In sharing this, I'm attempting to unveil how God slowly permeated my thinking with His thoughts in the midst of the suffering I was facing. He was working with skill and wisdom to bring me into alignment with His heart. This all culminated one day as I was listening to the radio. I heard a man share that when he was a young man, he would put his face in the dirt and pray, "God, humble me so that I know without You I am nothing but dirt." When I heard that prayer on the radio, something leapt within my heart! I had finally found the answer I was looking for. I lived in the countryside, and there were dirt fields all around me. I began going at night to a particular field, and, usually after a time of weeping, I would press my face into the dirt and pray, "Humble me so that I know without You I am nothing but dirt." Years have now passed, and all other prayers I prayed during those days have faded from my memory, as they made almost no impact on my soul. The only prayer I remember from this time period is "God, humble me so that I know without You I am nothing but dirt."

This prayer is a radical cry for humility. God used the suffering I experienced to evoke this plea in my heart. I became convinced that its fulfillment was my way out of the pain I was experiencing. In hindsight, it is so easy to see that this was the remnant grace of God at work, because this is not normal thinking (at least for me)! When you are in pain, the natural response is to ask God to take you out of it. I did this often throughout these years and tried anything I could to find a shortcut into healing. This request for humility is the opposite of a shortcut, but God is amazingly brilliant. He saw me in mediocrity and knew pride was destroying my life. He also knew that I did not have eyes to see it or ears to hear this painful truth. So rather than beating me over the head with it, He slowly and subtly planted His thoughts in my mind as I was seeking answers to the wounds of my heart. These thoughts ultimately birthed His desire within my emotions, and that is why I began to yearn to be emptied of pride. In the moment, I was disillusioned by the pain and could not comprehend why God would allow it. In hindsight, I see clearly that without it I would have never found the motivation to cast off the comfort of my deception and begin seeking for the treasure of humility.

I now attest that my intuition was correct. The fulfillment of this humility cry proved to be what liberated me from my pain.

What I did not know was that the path it would lead me down would be longer and more costly than what I could have imagined. Being completely honest, I would have never prayed that prayer if I knew what it was going to cost. Yet, I would not be who I am today had it not been for the raw moments of agonizing intercession when I cried out for the humility of heaven to possess me. Every child of God has a dangerous prayer woven into the fabric of his or her God-given identity. My hope is that the Spirit of God fans this into a flame of unfiltered, passionate expression. We serve a King with fire in His eyes (Revelation 19:12), and I desire to pray to Him with fire in mine because these are the prayers that He longs to answer.

CHAPTER THREE

The Hallmark of Pride

But he gives more grace. Therefore it says, "God
opposes the proud but gives grace to the humble."

———

JAMES 4:6

Pride is deceptively subtle; it has a blinding influence on
humanity. Though pride manifests uniquely in each person,
I have found there to be a universal hallmark consistently present
wherever pride exists. The presence of pride in a person's life can be
identified by an independent spirit. This phenomenon can be traced
back to the beginning of humankind. In Genesis, after humanity
and the earth were created, we find the story of "the fall." This is
referring to humankind's plunge into sin and separation from God.

Most people (Christian and non-Christian alike) are familiar with this story, but I have found that familiarity does not always equate with understanding. Viewing this scripture passage through the lens of an independence paradigm reveals truth that is often veiled in a casual reading.

Humankind was created to operate out of a place of childlike dependence upon God. When children are born into planet Earth, they are the most dependent of creatures. Children are completely incapable of providing for themselves and are in utter need of their parents for nutrients, affection, and care. In Luke 18:17, Jesus tells us, "Truly, I say to you, whoever does not receive the kingdom of God like a child shall not enter it." He is expressing that childlike dependence is crucial to kingdom living. Again in John 15, Jesus describes a relationship of dependence, this time using the analogy of a vine and its branches. He compares humanity to branches, which are utterly dependent upon the vine of Christ in order to bear fruit. This is the way humanity was designed to operate!

Adam and Eve came into the world having this type of relationship with God. In the garden, they walked and *talked* with God every day! They had never experienced anything other than a perfectly dependent, childlike union with God. His voice was their daily bread (as it should be), and they abided in it completely.

Deuteronomy 8:3 states, "He humbled you and let you hunger and fed you with manna, which you did not know, nor did your fathers know, *that he might make you know that man does not live by bread alone, but man lives by every word that comes from the mouth of the LORD*" (emphasis added). Israel's wilderness season was designed to use the Israelites' physical reliance on food as an outward display of their spirits' essential need for the voice of God. Communication is vital to all relationships, especially one with God. So many Christians confess that they rarely have connection with God's voice or that His voice is foreign to them altogether. This is the fruit of independence and is not what "normal" Christianity was intended to look like. We were designed for intimacy and hardwired by God for communication with Him. (It is worth noting that this communication is not limited to the Bible only but is governed by it. God will speak to us through all of creation, but He will not violate His revealed written word [Romans 1:20].) We were created for dependence on God—in practical terms, this looks like staying vitally connected to His voice (John 10:27). Like Jesus, we must be about our Father's business, doing only what we see Him at work doing (John 5:19).

Rewind to Genesis 3, where the serpent enters the scene in order to deceive Adam and Eve. The first words out of the serpent's mouth directly attack the woman's relationship with the voice of God. He begins, "Indeed, has God said?" (Genesis 3:1, question mark mine); then he proceeds to challenge God's commandment not to eat of the tree of knowledge of good and evil. The serpent is very crafty in this statement and is intentionally working to reveal another path that these humans can walk down, the path of independence! He appeals to their free will by proposing that they rely on themselves and trust in the power of human reason instead of walking in dependence upon God. This can seem so subtle in a casual reading of this passage, but we must understand how violent a grievance this is in the sight of God. In verse 5, the serpent tells the woman that when she eats the fruit she "will be like God." This statement captures the heart of independence—we act as our own gods. Adam and Eve both chose to eat the fruit, rejecting a relationship of trust and dependence on their Creator and choosing instead a path of human autonomy. In essence, they proclaimed to God, "We do not desire to live life your way; we will choose our own. We don't believe that you are good." This choice exemplifies independence and is a resounding hallmark of self-righteous pride. Operating in this paradigm results in decisions being made out of selfish human reason—disconnected from the voice, the wisdom, and the goodness of the Creator. This is why the world humanity has created is so riddled with pain and destruction. We chose to live life as "gods" and were manipulated into creating disorder. This is not what we were designed for!

In my life, independence masked itself with the lie "I don't need anyone but God." This led to a life of isolation where I became an island. No one, including God, had access to my heart, and no one was going to deter me from doing what I wanted. I lived in a self-absorbed ecosystem where I was the master of a universe that revolved around me. Despite how ugly this sounds, the disturbing truth is that this worked well for me. This actually works for a lot of people, Christian and non-Christian alike. Why? Because independence promises us control and allows each of us to act as our own god. Rehearsing the lie that we don't need anyone creates an ecosystem where we feel justified to remain in control.

For nearly a decade, I pursued athletics with a zeal beyond anyone I personally knew. My highest aim was to be a professional golfer. It was my dream and will for my life. I would be at the course until dark and be back up at the course again come sunrise. I was driven and highly motivated to make myself someone great, and golf was simply the tool I settled on using to do it. One day, when I was still a teenager, I heard the whisper of God as I was being driven to the golf course. "What if My will is not for you to be a professional golfer?" When this thought came into my mind, I was disturbed and vehemently tried to silence it. The whisper persisted, and again, I resisted: "That couldn't be God. I will be a professional golfer." That memory sums it all up for me. I was my own god. I was in control, and no one was going to get in the way of me doing what I thought was best for me, not even God.

Golf was eventually stripped from me, and I was completely devastated by this. Over time and by God's grace, my passion for golf was replaced with a passion for God. I became zealous for the word of God and prayer. In like manner to my relationship with golf, I began spending many late nights and early mornings seeking the Lord in prayer. This brought much fruit and transformation to my life because God is always faithful to our hearts. However, the truth is that the same unhealthy pattern of independence was still at play. I was still working really hard to manipulate God to align with my will and attempting to coerce Him into doing what I believed was best for my life. For the most part, this looked like really good things— ministry positions, promotions, relationships, etc.—but the underlying reality was that I was operating as the one in control. I viewed Christian spirituality as a method of achieving my own ambition.

I have been a Christian most of my life, yet I operated out of vile pride for many years. How is it possible to be a Christian and act as your own god at the same time? For me, it was through using Christian terms to spiritualize my selfishness. The lie I believed was "I don't need anyone *but God*," not, "I don't need anyone." Operating in this lie convinced me that the bad fruit in my life was not my fault. The addition of "but God" was added to ease my Christian conscience. Looking back, I can see many instances where I used the clause *but God* to cover up my selfishness and make it sound holy. I was blind to this while it was happening. Satan's schemes of pride and manipulation are so stealthy that they often go unnoticed. Pride is deceptively subtle and often hides in plain sight. It is only the love of Jesus that can remove the blinding veil of "spiritualized selfishness" and free us from this darkness.

As mentioned earlier, humankind was created to live in childlike dependence upon God. Contrary to what some believe, dependence upon God includes reliance upon other people as we all, together, form the Body of Christ. The truth is that we need each other desperately. We were not made to live life alone. Isolation is a cage of fear that torments the human soul. I've heard some people point to the ancient monastics as precedents for a life of spiritual independence and isolation, but this is an inaccurate statement. Even in monasticism, which values solitude and physical isolation, there was spiritual accountability woven into it at every level. Younger monks had older monks who served as spiritual fathers, bringing counsel and correction to them throughout their spiritual journeys. I highlight this in order to advocate that it is vital that you value and accommodate feedback in your life. If you are living devoid of outside voices who help you process, question, and evaluate decisions you are making, the chances are you are living in independence. This is because operating out of isolation makes us vulnerable to manipulation. We are far too easy on ourselves and are always able to justify our actions because we bathe our selfishness in good intentions (Proverbs 16:2). This is what leads to a paradigm of spiritualized selfishness. It is crucial that we have people in our lives who love us enough to call us out when they see discord between what we say and what we do. Even further, we must have people that we invite into our decision-making process itself, asking them to discern for themselves the motives, thoughts, and intentions behind our reasoning and rationale.

A number of months ago, I was meeting with a mentor that I process almost all crucial decisions with. I was explaining some of my plans for the future and why I believed God was leading me there. He prodded and asked a few questions that ultimately led him to gently suggesting that though these ideas seemed good, it seemed unnecessary to spend much time investing thought and energy into them in the current season. I was disturbed by his words and felt like he had "burst my bubble." Upon further reflection, I came to realize why I was so zealous to discuss these plans for the future. I was dealing with fear in my current circumstances, and these future plans were my escape route. My zeal was motivated by fear. If I had not processed this and invited my mentor into this vulnerable space, I would have acted upon these promptings (most likely in the name of being led by the Lord) and been outside the grace of God. Decisions made from fear will inevitably lead to disorder, no matter how good they appear initially. I would have never realized this without outside perspective. I cannot emphasize enough how much we need each other!

As Christians, we must come to accept that it is incongruent to claim to have an amazing walk with Jesus and at the same time boast a record of unfruitful actions that leave trails of tears, broken relationships, and disorder. Living in this dichotomy reveals the Word has not yet been made flesh in our lives. First John 4:20 is an incarnational litmus test that we can use to test the true quality of our spirituality. It reads, "If anyone says, 'I love God,' and hates his brother, he is a liar; for he who does not love his brother whom he has seen cannot love God whom he has not seen." This verse demonstrates that healthy relationships are paramount to Christian spirituality, as they reveal we truly love God!

Relationships operate as magnifying glasses that reveal hidden flaws within our hearts. They give opportunity for what is inside us to manifest, both good and bad. Pride and independence will always wreak havoc in relationships. It will be easy to discern their presence if we are willing to take an honest look at ourselves and discern the quality of our closest relationships.

My spiritual blindness was exposed and healed through an honest evaluation of my relationships. I had a recurring theme of broken relationships in my life—specifically, romantic relationships. A number of painful breakups left me wounded, feeling like I was a victim of bad luck and being treated unfairly. In my later university years, I was in a serious relationship that ended very suddenly and very painfully. It was a replay of a similar, painful dynamic that had taken place four years prior. My heart was shattered, and I was left trying to make sense of the circumstances. What added another layer of confusion was that I thought I had heard clearly from God that she was *the one*.

Before we continue, I want to pause and mention that I absolutely believe that God can and does at times tell people who their spouses will be. I view this not as a command but a Father's blessing—His affirmation of an affection that already exists and encouragement for His children to take a risk of love. In the case of my story, I was using "God told me" as an emotional crutch that gave me something to fall back on in case I got rejected, rather than a gift of inspiration to take a leap of faith into the unknown. John 7:17 reads, "If anyone's will is to do God's will, he will know whether the teaching is from God or whether I am speaking on my own authority." Here Jesus is linking self-surrender to God's will with the ability to discern whether someone is speaking of himself or of God. This verse holds significant insight into a healthy understanding of how to hear God's voice. Many people have authentic encounters with God but interpret these experiences incorrectly because they are not yet surrendered to the will of God. Selfish ambition is deafening and veils us from the voice of Jesus, causing us to manipulate His words in order to serve our own agendas. The closer something lies to our hearts and affections (like a romantic relationship), the more prone it is to being tampered with by selfish ambition. This is why self-surrender is so vital!

In retrospect, it is very clear to me that I wanted this young woman to be the one because I was lonely, in a lot of pain, and desperate for a relationship that could make me happy. I was vulnerable to the common form of emotional manipulation where you interpret anything God is saying to affirm what you want to hear. I wanted her to be the one, so I built my case on a series of emotional experiences. When I went back over my interpretation of these events years later, I realized that God was in fact speaking to me. But I took great liberty in the interpretation, which I arrived at independently of any outside voices, and that is what got me in trouble. This is a practical example of spiritualized selfishness. As this relationship came to a close, I was left broken and confused despite how much I was seeking the Lord. I questioned God's goodness, His reality, and my sanity in regard to hearing His voice. The ending of this relationship was a time of crisis. I began to feel very bad for myself and acted as if I was a martyr suffering for the sake of righteousness. I played through the circumstances of the relationship and began to rehearse stories that interpreted the events in my favor. This distanced me from having to take any ownership of the bad fruit clearly created.

I was seeking the Lord passionately and often in this season, and as I said before, no matter how broken we are, God is always faithful to our hearts. Despite the vulgar independence of my ways, He saw something good deep within me, and in His radical mercy, He spoke. I was sitting in a math class, disengaged from the teaching and replaying the circumstances in my head. My thinking began to wander back to past failed relationships, and in this train of thought, He whispered, "What is the common denominator?"

Much like when I was a teenager in the car on the way to the golf course, I recoiled at this whisper. I did not want to consider what He was asking. Again the thought raced through my mind, "What is the common denominator?" My gut wrenched, and almost instantly, I saw something that I had done my very best to bury. It was as if God brought me down to a closet in my soul where I had hidden something and made the decision to never return. His whisper was an invitation to go back and open the door. "What is the common denominator?" I knew the answer—it was me. I was the only common denominator in all these broken, painful events. The stories I had told myself were interwoven with the deception of pride, and the Lord was inviting me to come face to face with the truth.

This necessitated that I let go of the victim mindset I'd been using to excuse my actions. I had been through so much trauma at this point that it was easy to blame my poor behavior on the things that had happened to me. The truth is that we all fall victim to painful circumstances, but these circumstances do not have to define us. We each have a will and the ability to decide what to do with the pain we experience. Too many allow yesterday's trauma to steal from tomorrow's promise. I was sick of doing this because I realized it wasn't working. I chose to face my past, take ownership of my life and decisions, and actively pursue the healing of heaven. Doing this is what eventually liberated me from an endless cycle of perpetuating the same brokenness I had experienced.

Sitting in my statistics class in December of 2011, I resolutely said yes to God and let Him lead me to the closet where I had buried my pain and deepest fear. Though this was one of the scariest and most painful decisions I have ever made, I have no regrets about doing it. As I walked through this process of healing, I realized there was a deeper culprit at play. Independence is a nasty thing, but it is fed and supported by a greater enemy. It was time to face it head on and go to the root of the issue.

CHAPTER FOUR

A Deeper Culprit

There is no fear in love, but perfect love casts
out fear. For fear has to do with punishment, and
whoever fears has not been perfected in love.

―――

1 JOHN 4:18

I HAD STRUGGLED WITH INSECURITY MY ENTIRE LIFE. I NEVER admitted this to myself, but I was threatened by anyone whom I perceived to be more successful than me. There was an aching fear within my heart that I was simply not enough and that the desire for greatness within me was destined to be unsatisfied. Dating back to my earliest memories, I can recall a zeal to win and to use comparison to prove myself better than those around me. All my insecurities manifested in an insatiable desire to be the best. I don't think this desire is inherently bad, but it is a manipulation of a God-given desire for greatness. I looked for significance in comparison to others rather than deriving it from my Father, and that is idolatry. I would have told you my identity was "in Christ," but that was not true. Again referencing the incarnational litmus test, God's word must become flesh in us. We must actually bear fruit of what we profess to believe. I professed to find my identity in Christ, but I was driven like a madman to be the best at whatever I did so I could feel good about myself.

Insecurity and fear are inseparable from each other—they always run together. It should never be permissible for a Christian to accept that an insecure existence is tolerable. That is mockery to the cross of Jesus Christ. He died to set us free from fear by the power of His perfect love (1 John 4:18). Insecurity and fear form the foundation that pride is built upon. Once our fear is defeated, the house of pride will crumble! Another way of describing this is that independence is the external manifestation of pride. Like a weed that springs up in a garden bed, it's what pride looks like. However, expanding on this analogy, the hidden roots that support and nourish the whole plant are fear and insecurity. Any gardener knows that if you want to get rid of a weed, you have to uproot it! If you don't get the roots, the weed will grow back. It is no different with pride. Behavioral modification will not solve the issue, but will only morph pride's influence into another form. The only way to uproot pride is through a face-to-face confrontation with the often deep-rooted fear that plagues our hearts.

The process of discovering self-worth and identity in the eyes of the Father is not an overnight affair. Similarly, the process of peeling back the layers of insecurity and fear is not a quick process. The Lord had been at work in me for years, like an onion, removing layer after layer, preparing me for a deeper work of transformation. God works differently than we do. We want things to be instantaneous; God is deliberate in His timing. He spent five years preparing me to go to the place of raw confrontation with fear and insecurity because I would not have been ready for it otherwise. I want to share the journey as well as the breakthrough moment because the two should never be separated. If I only share the breakthrough, it discounts the process. The "mountaintop experience" of breakthrough is so much more majestic when you have spent yourself climbing the mountain of process. We often ask God, "Why is it so hard?" in the midst of the painstaking labor of process. The answer is that He knows us, He loves us, and He wants us to experience the joy that comes only through hard work. There are no shortcuts in the kingdom. We have to climb the mountain with Him.

I grew up in a home full of hidden trauma. We incur trauma in two different ways: when hurtful things are done to us and when necessary things are withheld from us. My home was characterized by the latter. I thought the lack of intimacy and affection in my home was normal; such is the case for many who experience this. The result was a void in my heart that I sought desperately to fill.

In the vacuum created by this trauma, a paradigm of performance flourished. I mentioned earlier that I often lashed out in pain against my younger brother when we were growing up. My behavior was beyond that of normal sibling scuffles. The ugliness of my words and actions went so far that they destroyed our relationship. This was in many ways caused by growing up in a performance paradigm that forced us to compete to garner recognition, affirmation and ultimately self-esteem. Due of the lack of male affection in our home, we both were trying our best to "win" as much as we could. I, being the oldest, would most often come out "on top". This ugly dynamic caused so much pain and division, but the worst part is we thought this was "normal life". Though this seemed normal to us, God was not satisfied

When I went away to college, Riley began to flourish, mostly because of the work God began doing in his life and partly because I was out of the picture for the first time. He began to be the bright light that garnered attention and recognition. He began stepping into the authority of who he is. To a certain degree, this was threatening to me, but being in different states and in completely different spheres, it was not something I gave a lot of thought to. One Christmas break, the Lord chose to pull off this scab in my heart and began to deal with the dysfunction at play between us. My mother, Riley, and I were praying in our living room, and while in prayer, I heard the Lord clearly tell me, "Wash your brother's feet and tell him you will serve him and live to make him better than you."

I was immediately struck with an intense wave of vulnerability. "Better than me" was not language I used for anyone. This command violated my insecure paradigm and exposed an orphan mindset that had influenced all of my life up until that point. The orphan mindset, also referred to by some as a poverty mindset, is when you live governed by scarcity. If you have any familiarity with the world of economics, you know that the underlying principle that drives all economic behavior is that of scarcity. There is only so much resource in the world, and humans are bound to an endless tug-of-war over who will get the limited supply. More simply put, there are only so many pieces of pie, and if you want one, you will have to fight for it!

I learned this in my pursuit of a professional golf career. My goal for nearly a decade was to be on the PGA Tour. I was haunted every day of that journey by the uncomfortable truth that out of the hundreds of thousands of people who shared my dream, only a few hundred actually saw that dream materialize. There was a real scarcity of opportunity at play! This created a drive in me that was unrelenting and extremely unhealthy. I could never rest because I had banked my whole identity on something extremely hard to achieve. As I mentioned earlier, by God's grace I had this dream stripped away. This triggered a severe identity crisis that ended up pushing me into the arms of the Father. I converted from a life of worshipping a small white ball to one seeking after the living God. This was good in many regards, but I still found myself fighting for my slice of the pie.

I began to study church history and revival literature and learn about the people God had used to do great things. I still found my significance through comparison, so I began to be haunted over the idea that there were only so many powerful callings "out there." The irony is that in a gospel that promotes humility, it's very difficult to justify wanting to be used for greatness at the expense of other people being used in lesser measure. I would ask, "Does God destine some men to do small things and others to be used for great things?" I witnessed so much mediocrity in the Body of Christ that I became terrified I was destined for it myself. The same scarcity mindset was at play. I was attributing to God's economy the nature of the world's economy. I genuinely believed, because of what I had experienced in the church, that there were only so many powerful callings "out there," and I was torn between wanting to fight for my slice of the pie and at the same time surrender.

God used that night with Riley to begin what was for me a long process of repentance from this toxic scarcity mindset. Repentance is the process of renouncing the lies God exposes and turning to embrace the truths He reveals instead. This is how transformation takes place. That night, I was caught in a wrestling match, knowing I had heard from God but adamantly opposed what He was asking me to do. My thoughts were racing. "How can I live to make him better than me if there is already such a scarcity of callings? This does not bode well for my pursuit of 'success'!" These thoughts revealed that my mind was governed by poverty thinking, which ultimately was the fear that God had created me with desires He was not able to satisfy.

The truth is that our world is governed by scarcity, but His kingdom is not. He is a God of abundance and has fullness attached to every single one of His children. In His economy, there is room for everyone to be powerful, fulfilled, and significant. There is no shortage of callings. There is no scarcity of anointing. There is no one else you would ever want to be. We live in a world full of brokenness and pain, and we are the answer. There are more than seven billion powerful callings waiting to be realized in the earth today, and each one is great. Mediocrity is the fruit of living in fear, not the ordained will of God. Every child dreams a great dream because they were hand-made in the image of a great God. We have permission to ask Him for greatness; it is in our DNA.

When I speak of greatness, I mean from His perspective, not necessarily from ours. The greatest moment in human history was when an obscure Middle-Eastern man with a small following was put to death outside a remote city in the hills of Judea. Many travelers passed by the scene, most likely veering to the other side of the road to avoid the shameful mess of the crucifixion. What disgusted humankind captivated all of heaven. The fate of cosmic history was in the balance, and Jesus succeeded. He breathed His last breath painfully after solemnly proclaiming, "It is finished." This is victory incarnate. I am, of course, referring to Jesus's sacrifice on the cross, where He wrought eternal redemption on behalf of humanity.

Eternity defines greatness differently than mortals do. Heaven will not marvel over how many people came to your church, how much money you gave to charity, or even how many people you led to Christ. What will be honored is the way that you loved. The true measure of a human is love. Love never fails, in this life or the one that follows. We were made to impact eternity, and this will only be fulfilled if we learn to love. Businesses, governments, ministries, and worldly influence will all pass away at death, but love remains. For that reason, greatness is not measured by the size of your platform or how much influence and notoriety you garner. This life is a mere breath when compared to the scope of eternity. Greatness is a life that breaks past the confines of mortal existence and leaves a legacy that echoes in the life to come. This is only accomplished through love, and that is what God wills for each of us to become.

It is very easy for me to identify the greatest person I have ever met: it's my mom. She is not famous, doesn't have a very large following, and waited forty years to see God's calling to be a pastor fulfilled. What makes her great is the love she exudes. It marks people deeply. I have been astounded by her, as she has no desire to be the one in the spotlight but gets her joy from loving people deeply. My life is the fruit of her love. Her fingerprints will be on every page of my story. It will be my joy to carry her legacy to the next generation. She has taught me what greatness truly consists of. This is the type of life we all were created to live.

Back to my story where I was to wash Riley's feet. I eventually consented and obeyed the Lord. I washed my brother's feet and, with sorrow in my heart, told him I was sorry for how I had treated him. I then forced myself to speak the words, "I will serve you and live to make you better than myself." I knew it was a covenantal moment, and it was hard for me to swallow. I want to be very clear: I felt no goosebumps or spectacular sensations as I did this. We do not live by feelings; we live by faith. I meant what I said, but my emotions were in turmoil. Too many times, I have heard people say things like, "I just don't have peace" or "I don't feel led" as a cop-out of sobering obedience. Obedience does not always feel good, but it always creates good.

Throughout the following years there were many moments where the Lord would remind me of my commitment to my brother and in times of his exalting, ask me, "Will you rejoice in his achievement? Will you celebrate his success? Will you live to make him better than you?" This rubbed me raw many times, but I began to notice my heart changing. My emotions began to align, though years later, with the words I had confessed. The Word was becoming flesh in me. I can tell you now that the thought of seeing him shine literally makes me cry tears of joy. God put His heart inside me, and it's not just for my brother, but for all that He has called me to lead and serve.

Continuing on into the repentance journey, God was relentlessly at work in me. He would almost constantly bring me into orchestrated experiences that exposed some form of fear and insecurity, requiring that I get my hands dirty digging for answers. I learned in this season that repentance is not complete until you have understanding of an issue. You have to dig down into the roots of problems so you can literally "stand under" the whole ecosystem and uproot the mindset. Coming into understanding is what clears space for truth to be implanted.

I was visiting a powerful church, and as I watched the pastor minister in the power of God, I couldn't help but think, "God could never use me like that." The voice of insecurity often sounds humble, but it keeps us in bondage. For the rest of the day, I felt very vulnerable and was struggling with shame. I was praying and processing for the next day, asking God why on earth I felt so miserable. I was seeking understanding. I began to journal, and the Lord spoke to me: "You need to repent of your self-righteous pride." He then continued, "You think far too highly of your insecurities. Do not tell me what I can and cannot do. He (the powerful pastor) is a man, just like you are a man. If I can use him, I can use you. Repent of your pride before My face." I was stunned and convicted. I thought the sentiment I had expressed was humble, when in fact it was extremely selfish. In essence, I was proclaiming to God that I believed my sin and brokenness were more powerful than the atoning blood of Jesus Christ that was shed on the cross. When I looked at it in this light, I began to recognize that the little excuses I often made for my shortcomings, such as "I'm no saint" or "I'm just a sinner," were exceedingly self-righteous when brought directly before God. He made Jesus sin, who knew no sin, so that we would become the righteousness of God (2 Corinthians 5:21), and that we are! There are many voices seeking to tell us who we are in this life—shame, doubt, insecurity, performance, and lust all have something to say to us. In all of this, we must choose to agree with the blood of Jesus that cries out on our behalf, calling us righteous and redeemed!

God was exposing false-humility within me, which, in the same way as independence, is fed by insecurity and fear. I was step by step coming into understanding of the thoughts that plagued my life and stole from my God-given inheritance. These two stories are small snapshots into an extended process that prepared the soil of my heart to receive a deep experience of sanctifying grace. *Sanctification* is a term used to describe the process of becoming holy like Jesus. It is often confused with a notion of human moral perfection, which it is far from. Sanctification is not about striving for perfection, but about surrendering to the work of the cross. God forms and fashions us into His likeness; we simply learn to yield to the Potter's hands. Sanctification is both a powerful experience and an ongoing process. We do not ever "arrive" in this life, yet there are moments when God accomplishes something mighty inside of us. I compare it to when a wild mustang finally is broken to its master. Though the mustang may have moments of backsliding and is required to continue in submission, something resolute takes place when the wildness is broken. Fear and the pride it fosters are a wildness that God resolutely breaks in the sanctification experience. It is a true taste of death, but even more, an overwhelming, exponential release of life.

Returning to the day in my math class when God had asked me, "What is the common denominator (in the broken relationships)?" I described it as feeling as though God was bringing me to a closet that I had done my best to never revisit. It was finally time to turn the handle and face what was inside. I felt sick to my stomach, but I opened the door, and what I saw left me heartbroken. I was taking an honest look at the string of broken relationships in my life, and I finally had eyes to perceive the truth of my behavior. When I looked, all I could see was selfishness. The vision I had as a seventeen-year-old—the one at which I had screamed to God, "Don't let me go down that path!"—was my reality. Insecurity was driving my life, and no matter how good the intentions of my heart, my love was infected with fear. I was so insecure that everything I did for other people came with an unspoken expectation of my needs being met.

The Lord showed me that I was like a self-righteous peacock, and that anytime I felt afraid, I would simply strut my feathers and go over the top to earn love. I'd spent my whole life trying to earn affection by being the best. In relationships, anytime I felt vulnerable to rejection, I would start going over the top in acts of kindness and affection. This looked loving, but it wasn't pure. It wasn't the love of God because I was at the center of it. My "love" had strings attached to it in the form of needs that I demanded be met, and when they weren't, I would be appalled. I would think things like, "I am doing all this for you, and you have the audacity to do/withhold _____!" As this pattern continued, I felt I was justified in lashing out in anger. Time and time and time again, it was all about me, and seeing this broke me. I saw the wounds my blindness had caused. I saw the hypocrisy evident in my spirituality. I felt like nothing and nobody.

I was in worship at church one day, and I had a vision where the Lord spoke very gently to me and revealed a very hard truth that finally brought me into a place of understanding. He showed me a picture of the cross, bloodstained and beautiful. I was standing on top of it. He told me, "You've seen people as if they were ladders, things upon which to climb. You would have used anything and anyone to lift yourself up, including the cross of My Son." I was on the ground of the church weeping for a very long time because it was true. I was a master manipulator, and I did it all with a heart full of good intentions. I had used many people to try to make me feel good about myself. This wasn't in the form of sinful acts, but ministry laced with my own agenda. On the outside, I looked like a giver (of encouragement, wisdom, counsel, etc.), but on the inside, I was a taker. I was doing it all with a hidden agenda of making myself feel special and valuable. Selfish ambition always has an agenda. We have to recognize that this infects our love and good intentions and turns them putrid. It's like mixing a small amount of urine into a glass of pure water. Even though it's 95 percent pure, the whole glass is contaminated.

This contamination took place because I did not know my worth. I had no idea whether I was valuable or not. The root of it all was a lie that I had built my whole life upon: "You have no inherent value." This lie is the voice of shame. Believing this to be true is extraordinarily painful and fractures our identity. To safeguard our hearts from experiencing this pain, we employ fear to "protect" us. This is what creates the hamster wheel of performance and striving. I fell victim to it all. I believed I was what I could do, and therefore every achievement I had zealously striven for throughout my life was an attempt to ease the agony of shame buried deep within my heart. I was attempting to prove by my performance that I had value.

I realized that fear was the strong man that insured shame had a place of residence within me. My pursuit of understanding finally had bottomed out. I could stand under the whole plant of pride and at last was positioned to have it uprooted from my life. Independence is the fruit that the plant of pride bears in our lives. Fear and insecurity are the influences that govern our thinking and make up the stem and root system of the plant. And lastly, the seed that causes the plant of pride to germinate within us is shame, the lie that we have no value and are worth only what we can do. As I previously wrote, understanding positions us to fully remove a lie and then fully receive truth. The truth is that the message of shame is a hoax. We have worth at our lowest and darkest place.

In Ephesians 1:18, Paul prays that the eyes of our hearts will be opened and by wisdom and revelation be able to perceive three things. One of these three things is that we would know the riches of His glorious inheritance in the saints. In other words, that we will know our worth to God. The universal answer to the question, "What is my value?" is that we are worth what we were paid for, the precious blood of Jesus. However, we must come to deeply, intimately, and experientially know this truth if we are to be set free from the bondage of fear and shame.

God answers this prayer in the valleys of life, not on the mountaintops. We are so conditioned to perform that God, in His wisdom, knows the only place we can comprehend the unconditional nature of His love is in the places where it wasn't earned or deserved. This is God's method of rendering shame void and exposing it as false.

Humility is knowing exactly who you are without Christ, and exactly who you are in Christ at the same time. During this season, God answered my prayer to know that without Him I am nothing but dirt. This by definition requires a sojourn down into the valley. I experienced who I was without Christ, and it was death to my flesh. During these painful days, I went to the beach one afternoon. It was wintertime, so it wasn't crowded, but people were still scattered here and there around me. I was walking alone when a wave of grief suddenly crashed over me. I fell on my knees, put my face in the sand, and almost instinctively began chewing the coarse grains of sand, grinding them relentlessly against my teeth. (You are probably thinking, "This guy has lost his mind!" I was thinking the same thing.) As hard as it is to explain, this wasn't an act of madness, but rather an act of prayer. I was doing my best to externalize the emotions of my soul. As I chewed upon the awful, grainy texture, I found comfort. I didn't care that people around me thought I looked crazy. I didn't care what anybody thought, for that matter.

What I found through this experience is that something very powerful takes place when we take our pain before God in authentic and raw expression. We have permission to communicate our turmoil to Him. This is called lament. True lament does not take place from a bitter heart, but from a heart experiencing loss and yet still hoping in God. Jeremiah lamented the loss of Jerusalem and recorded that he too ground his teeth like gravel (Lamentations 3:16), yet he did not lose hope in the process (Jeremiah 29). On this unremarkable winter afternoon, I was grieving the loss of my life in the face of all the hopes I had had for it.

After a time, I picked my head up and began staring intently toward heaven. My mouth was full of spit and sand, and I felt like a complete idiot. Despite this, in an unexplainable way, I knew heaven was responding to me. In hindsight, I know this was when God answered the prayer I had prayed several years earlier. He humbled me so that I would know without Him I am nothing but dirt. I actually experienced it during those few minutes. When you go to places that low, you can never forget. It's been more than six years since that day, and it's as real to me now as it was then. It left me marked and painfully aware of how desperately I need God. The wildness in me died that afternoon. It was replaced with a sincere and holy fear of the Lord. I am nothing apart from Him.

This is not the end of the story, nor is it the reason why I share this brief collection of events that together chronicle my deconstruction process. I've brought you into the valley of my journey because it was here that Paul's prayer to know our worth was answered for me. I was writhing in the reality of my shame, receiving revelation of who I am outside of the grace and mercy of Jesus. Though this was highly unpleasant, it formed the foundation upon which I could begin to learn who I am in His eyes.

The idea that God loves me was not a new concept. This is a widely confessed statement. It had been rehearsed to me countless times throughout my life, but it was not real to me. In Ephesians

3:19, Paul prays that we would *know* the love of Christ that surpasses knowledge, that we might be filled to all the fullness of Christ. The word *know* in the Greek is *ginosko,* meaning, "to know." In the Greek Septuagint, the Hebrew word *yada,* meaning, "to know" is replaced by the Greek word *ginosko* throughout the Old Testament. So you could say they are synonyms of a kind. What's the big deal? In Greek thought, knowledge was associated with the intellect. Reason and logic were king. The Greeks pioneered what is known today as Western thought, which is the philosophical paradigm that ushered in the age of modernity and science. None of this is wrong; it is simply different from the Hebrew worldview.

Hebrews viewed knowledge as something gained through experience. In Genesis 2, we see the verse that Adam knew *(yada)* Eve and she conceived a son. This isn't referring to the intellect, but to a very intimate and experiential knowledge! This is important because the author of Ephesians 3 is the Hebrew man Paul of Tarsus. When he writes his prayer that we would know the love of Christ, he is *not* referring to our intellect. The knowledge he is speaking of surpasses the intellect; it can only be known through intimate experience. In other words, we must know in the heart what the head can never comprehend.

I take time to explain this because the church in modernity has looked down upon the idea of subjective revelation and personal experience in regard to relationship with Jesus Christ. Stereotypically speaking, Western Christianity has valued only what could be proved by logic and reason. This is one of the major shifts taking place in the postmodern church today. Science and reason have been exposed as insufficient to save humanity from violence, war, and injustice. This has served to awaken people to the undeniable reality that there is something more than what we are able to perceive with our five senses. The spiritual realm is active among us. This is not just inside Christianity, but pervasive of all culture.

The Church of Jesus Christ must realign with the Word of God as it pertains to the mystical nature of the gospel. We cannot read a Bible laced with angelic visitation, prophetic revelation, and supernatural manifestations of God's healing power and then denounce all personal experience as wrong and dangerous. Nearly every biblical character's story started with a personal experience with the living God. Abraham heard a voice, David received a prophecy from Samuel, Moses saw a burning bush, Gideon beheld an angel, Daniel and Ezekiel had visions, Joseph had a dream, Paul was blinded on the road to Damascus, Cornelius had an angelic visitation—the list can go on and on! If they needed an encounter with God, so do we. All experience must be held up to the Word for its validation, interpretation, and application. However, we must recognize that the Word grants permission not only to have these experiences, but to seek them.[5] This is not to say that we throw out spiritual discipline, biblical exegesis, and sound theology, but that in all these things we leave room to experience God Himself. All of our study must lead us to a personal knowledge of Jesus. If our study does not transform us into His image, then in the end, it is fruitless. Our highest goal should not be to know the Bible, but to know the Author!

The love of God is not to be known as a noble and novel thought; it is to be powerfully and intimately experienced. One encounter with the love of Jesus and a life is forever transformed. I am a firsthand witness and living example of this. I was raised in the church my entire life, and it was not until I was twenty-one years old that I finally realized I was loved. We each must have our own revelation of what His love means for us. Any good parent will agree with this. My mom loves each of her boys with a very special love—my brothers and I have never doubted this—yet at the same time, each of our relationships with her looks very different. She loves us each uniquely and, in doing so, demonstrates that she knows us for who we are. God's love is even greater. We are all formed as one of a kind and therefore have different needs and means of receiving love. God formed us to fill these deep desires for Himself, and He fully intends to do so.

God uniquely revealed His love for me through two very different but profound experiences. They happened a little more than two years apart from each other but I will share them both because they are two sides of the same coin. The first encounter is incomplete without the second, and vice versa. In one, I experienced power and in the other, mercy. God is thorough in His dealings.

The first was a visitation in the form of a vision. It happened three times before I processed what was happening (I was not familiar or comfortable with this sort of thing). In the vision, I was running through a barren desert at night. I was being chased by a pack of wolves howling into the darkness. I was breathing heavily and consumed with fear. Each time the howls sounded, I could feel a cold shiver flow through my body. I instinctively knew what the wolves were—lust, addiction, depression, fear, torment—all the things that had haunted me for the last several years of my life. I was running to escape them, but was all too aware that I could not, no matter how hard I tried. A couple times, I fell from exhaustion onto the cold desert floor, but fear would seize my body, and I'd get up and keep running. Eventually, I ran out of steam. My body gave out, and I collapsed onto the ground trembling as the howls grew louder and closer. I waited in agony, flinching in anticipation of all my fears overtaking me and becoming an inescapable reality. This was a living portrait of my life—though it was only a vision, it felt more real than reality. As I continued watching the vision play out, the wolves began to close in on me, howling in disordered chaos. I wanted to close my eyes, but couldn't. Just as they were about to leap on me and tear me apart, everything changed.

Two giant paws stepped over my little body, and a light broke forth like a lightning bolt. The most massive lion I had ever seen stood over me with a mane that looked like white fire. He roared into the darkness, and it sounded like a thundering waterfall. In His roar, He said only two words, but they changed me for all eternity: "He's Mine!" As I watched and heard this vision, the love of God literally consumed me in a way I did not know was possible. It was as though untouched and long-neglected crevices of my soul were filled with the most indescribable, joyful, and overwhelming goodness. Light consumed the darkness, and I watched the wolves turn and run away in horror. I belonged to Jesus. I was claimed by a King. Those two words, "He's Mine," literally became my identity. Every time I ponder this experience—even now, writing about it—the love is fresh. I reexperience it. I get emotional talking about it. I fell so deeply in love with Jesus, the Lion of Judah, and I have never recovered. In that moment, I *"yada"* He loved me.

Days passed, and I was left to try and make sense of this experience. I was honestly overwhelmed by it and had much to process. I value authenticity greatly, and so I wanted to be sure what I had experienced was of God. One test I use to determine the validity of subjective encounters is the fruit that they bear. I first make sure they align with the principles of scripture; this one certainly did, but sometimes you are still left to question if it was simply your own imagination at work. To discern this, I look to what effect an experience has upon my real, flesh-and-blood, often unremarkable everyday life. If a personal experience brings positive transformation, you can know with surety that you have encountered God.

After my vision of the Lion, I was radically different. Depression was dispelled from me, and I have not dealt with it since. My countenance changed. My heart changed. I began to experience hope and had renewed passion. I found myself perpetually starving to enter into the presence of God. All I knew was that I wanted to be with Him. I was in university at the time, and a psychology professor whom I had no personal connection with outside of class wrote me to tell me that she noticed something very profound had happened during the course of the semester. She said she could notice it just in the way I was sitting in class. I was visibly different, even to a casual observer! This experience was amazing, but it was not the culmination. The Father still had something more to show me.

This was because despite how powerful the encounter was, something within me believed that somehow I had earned this "special experience." Because pride had not yet been uprooted, it infected this holy experience with its decaying influence. It perverted my thoughts and fed my ego. I used it to compare myself to others, and that made me feel significant. My revelation of being the beloved was still incomplete.

My second experience with His love was quite different from the first. This one took place a couple years after my encounter with the Lion and only days after my experience chewing the sand at the beach. I had been in so much pain that I wasn't sleeping well. I would often fall asleep either in tears or on the verge of them and then wake up with a pit in my stomach. I was still overwhelmed by the shame of seeing how flagrant my sin was, despite how hard I'd been trying to seek God. I went to sleep one afternoon sick to my stomach, and I awoke with the most secure sense of serenity emanating inside me. I was expecting the pit in my stomach, and instead, I found a spring of peace. I was literally flabbergasted. I kept touching my chest and my stomach as if I were trying to touch what I was feeling. I quickly put on some clothes and made my way to the prayer chapel that served as my little sanctuary during my university years. I sat before the Lord and asked Him to tell me what was going on. I knew it was good, but I didn't understand it.

He then spoke and said to me, "Jordan, I know this has been death to you, and it was supposed to be. I could not let you continue in the sins of your fathers, and your fathers' fathers, and your fathers' fathers' fathers. I came and set you free." At these words, my eyes were opened to the immense mercy of God. I had been crying for freedom for years at that point, all the while walking in the blindness of my pride. In this moment, I realized how exceedingly patient God had been toward me. He believed in me even when I was walking in flagrant violation of His will and causing all kinds of pain to others because of it. He did not despise me when I was living as a victim, comforting myself with the story that I was suffering for righteousness's sake when in truth I was being disciplined for my pride. Rather, He bestowed favor upon me in my selfishness. He lavished me with goodness and blessing in my brokenness. He came and roared, "He's Mine" when I was His enemy, not His friend. I was His beloved long before He was mine.

His love was never conditional upon my behavior, but upon His belief in who I am. His faith in me, and in all of us, is profound. He is love and so believes all things, hopes all things, and endures all things. I still cannot wrap my head around how He was able to see good in me through all the smoke and mirrors of selfishness and manipulation. I recognized that this love had nothing to do with my behavior and performance. I recognized that everything that had happened had been designed by love, and it wrecked me because I had done nothing to earn it! In fact, I had done everything possible to disqualify myself from it, and my efforts fell short! God's mercy triumphed over judgment. I had finally come to grips with the truth that I deserved punishment, and in that very place, He showed me mercy.

I equate it to the woman caught in the act of adultery who was thrown at the feet of Jesus. She was exposed and guilty. A heap of shame dropped before the Holy One, she undoubtedly was left trembling in anticipation of the stones that were soon to be hurled. Instead, she received the mercy of Jesus. He turned the valley of Achor, a place of just punishment (Joshua 7:24), into a door of hope (Hosea 2:15). When you receive mercy in the valley, it breaks you because you're forced to recognize that the punishment you deserved was given to someone else. The stones that fell silently next to the adulterous woman would morph into whips and fists beating Jesus a short time later. I am that adulterous woman, and the punishment that brought me peace fell upon Him. The love of Jesus far surpasses anything of this world, and all I can say is that it changed me once I *knew* it. He bestows grace and favor on weak, selfish people and loves us in our brokenness. We were His beloved long before He was ours.

Through this, Jesus lifted the veil of pride that had blinded me, at last setting me free to live the abundant life He created me for. I do not claim to possess any sort of immunity from pride, as that would be foolishness. Rather, I now have an acute awareness of it and perceive the ploys and tactics that come against me. My eyes are wide open. Like I mentioned earlier, I was a wild horse that finally broke. It was not force that broke me; it was His mercy, and it changed me profoundly. I've heard it said that when you get to the end your life, you step into His. This has been my experience.

I have discovered that His intentionality is without equal. He sees the end from the beginning, and every act He performs has purpose beyond what we can initially comprehend. When He breaks, it is so He can build, and when He wounds, it is so He can heal. I learned much in the breaking, yet I have now learned even more in the years that have followed. The newfound freedom I received liberated me to partner with the creative force of God's Spirit to see the mandate to create begin to be fulfilled in my life. The learning curve on this is steep and long but endlessly thrilling. Learning to walk with God is the greatest thing we could ever do. One day of abiding is better than a thousand days of striving!

I pray that as many of you have read these chapters, God has begun a deeper work of grace in you. I pray that you will continue to yield your heart more fully and allow God to complete what He has started. With that being said, it is time to shift gears to the journey up. God is building a kingdom, and we are his co-laborers. There is much He desires to accomplish through us, and the foundation is a humble, broken, and contrite heart (Psalm 51:17).

PART TWO

"And a Time to Build"

Ecclesiastes 3:3

INTRO PART TWO

W HAT YOU HAVE READ UP TO THIS POINT WAS THE BREAKING-
down process of the pride that kept me from abiding in Christ.
It took all of that unwinding and unlearning to get me to the place
where I could start the process of growing up in God. The revelation
of His love for me and who I am in His eyes is the ABCs of the gospel.
His love is the foundation for all that we are and all that we do in the
kingdom of God. The last years since His love took hold of me have
been exceedingly fruitful and remarkably humbling. My eyes have
repeatedly been opened to how little I know and how great my need
for Him is.

In 1 Corinthians, Paul famously writes, "Where the Spirit of the
Lord is, there is freedom." This gift of liberty is the greatest thing
I received through the years of breaking and humbling. God came
and set me free. Paul goes on to relate that the freedom we are given
is to behold the face of Jesus and be transformed into His image, from
one degree of glory to another (1 Corinthians 3:17)! John the Beloved
uses the word *abide* to describe this same idea. We are free to live in
union with God.

Abiding in Christ is the paramount discipline of New Testament
spirituality. It is the work involved in learning how to remain in the
love of God (John 15:9). We do not work to earn His love; we work to
stay rooted and grounded within it. Learning to abide is the process

of growing up in Christ. Another term closely linked to abiding is *co-laboring*. When I use this, I am speaking of working from a place of union with Christ. Abiding is the foundation that co-laboring is built upon. Abiding practically focuses on the disciplines involved in growing your prayer life, while co-laboring describes the fruit that these disciplines create in the real world. These are both terms that capture different aspects of the divine-human partnership between God and His children.

God is looking for mature partners in the family business of bringing heaven to earth. As it is in the natural, so it is in the spiritual. Our earthly fathers train us throughout our lives with the goal of entrusting more and more responsibility to us as we demonstrate the fruit of maturity. It is no different with God. The invitation to co-labor with God is the most exciting and purposeful opportunity imaginable. God is asking us to join Him at work. No job can compare to this one. The star-breather and universe architect wants us to help Him fulfill His glorious purposes on earth. The God who confidently tells us nothing is impossible for Him desires our help—this makes me giddy just thinking about it!

God created us with purpose and put a God-sized dream within us. These dreams will only be fulfilled through the divine-human partnership of co-laboring. God never intended that we would do it alone. He created life to be an adventure that we would face and overcome together. He simply loves our company. We must understand that even when we reach full maturity, we are still junior partners in this relationship. He is the miracle worker, and each of us His choise vessel. He is the master soloist, and each of us a violin in His hand. It is the most joyful of situations; it is hard to fathom how highly favored we are.

Though our role in the co-laboring partnership may be small compared to God's, we have a role to play nonetheless. We are given freedom and responsibility and must steward this well if we are to be entrusted with more. He is a good Father and passionate about empowering His children. His will is that we will bear much fruit (John 15:8).

CHAPTER FIVE

Co-Laborers with Christ

I am the vine, you are the branches; he who
abides in Me and I in him, he bears much fruit,
for apart from Me you can do nothing.

———

JOHN 15:5

J ESUS WALKED THIS EARTH AS A LIVING DEPICTION OF WHAT IT LOOKS like to abide in God. Hebrews 1:3 tells us that Jesus "is the radiance of His glory and the exact representation of His nature." In John 14, Jesus gets upset when Phillip asks Him to reveal the Father and replies back, "Have I been so long with you, and yet you have not come to know Me, Phillip? He who has seen Me has seen the Father."

Jesus asserts this so confidently because of the way He chose to live His life. He emptied Himself of His divinity and became obedient to the Father to the point of death (Philippians 2:8). In other words, He demonstrated what it looks like for a man to live in perfect, unbroken communion with the Father. I want to make something exceedingly clear: Jesus was, is, and always will be God. He chose not to play the God card while walking on earth in order to conquer sin as the second Adam (i.e., a man). Hebrews 2:7 tells us He is a merciful high priest because He was tempted in all things as we are, yet without sin. At the same time, James 1:13 says that God cannot be tempted. Jesus did not walk through the wilderness season of tempting as God; He did so as a man. He could have taken up His divine power at any moment, as He was and is fully God, but He *chose* not to.

Kenotic Christology is the theological term for what I am speaking about. *Kenosis* is the Greek term used in Philippians 2 for "emptied." Jesus willingly emptied Himself of His divine status so He could be the Savior and Sanctifier of humanity. Jesus came to demonstrate what life was intended to look like. He walked in power and purity and told us to do likewise. In Matthew 5, He tells us to be perfect as our Heavenly Father is perfect. In John 12, Jesus explains that we, his disciples, will do greater works (miracles) than He did. The very name *Christians,* "little anointed ones," denotes that we are to be like Christ. We are to follow Him and become like Him.

None of this makes sense unless Jesus's life was a model for what it looks like for a human to walk with God. If He lived His life, walked in purity, healed the sick, and loved unto death while operating in His divinity as God, it is unreasonable for Jesus to tell us to do the same, because we are completely unable! Contrastingly, if Jesus was limited in His humanity as we are and was simply a yielded vessel the Holy Spirit flowed through, we have hope that being Christlike is in the realm of possibility.

All throughout the Gospel of John, Jesus gives clear insight into the nature of His relationship with the Father. He makes statements that give greater credence to Paul's words in Philippians 2. I will list a few below and encourage you to do your own study of John's gospel.

John 5:19: "Truly, truly I say to you, the Son can do nothing of Himself, unless it is something He sees the Father doing."

John 5:30: "I can do nothing on My own initiative. As I hear, I judge, and My judgment is just, because I do not seek My own will, but the will of Him who sent Me."

John 8:27: "I do nothing on My own initiative, but I speak these things as the Father taught Me."

These statements make clear that Jesus had emptied Himself of His divine privileges and become a servant fully yielded to the will of God. When Jesus says He can do nothing on his own accord, He really means nothing!

Critics of this teaching claim it's dangerous, mainly for two reasons. First, they claim, this denies Jesus His deity, and secondly, it casts humans as far too powerful. I have already addressed the first claim. Jesus was, is, and always will be God. His emptying took place when He chose to leave the realms of heaven to take on the nature of a man and embrace the role of a servant. This manifested as a minute-to-minute choice to surrender as He walked the earth for the sake of humanity. Jesus had emotions that were contrary to the Father's will, yet He always chose to yield. In the Garden of Gethsemane, He pleaded, "Father, If you are willing, take this cup from me; yet not my will, but yours be done" (Luke 22:42). This verse captures that Jesus Himself was desiring not to go the cross, but He chose to listen to the Father because He had surrendered fully, even to the point of death. This does not rob Jesus of His divinity, but demonstrates His humanity. Jesus could have played His "God card" anytime while on earth, because He was and is God! He could have thrown Himself off the temple mount and had the angels catch Him if He desired it (Luke 4:9). However, Jesus *chose* not to because it would have defeated the Father's purpose in sending Him to break the curse of sin on behalf of mankind. Jesus is fully God and fully man, the eternal Word made flesh and bone.

Now to address the second concern—that this teaching presents humans as far too powerful. I have found that many perceive the power of God through a lens of triumphalism. What I mean by this is that we perceive the vessels God flows through as if they are generals of conquering armies, possessing great power and having the authority to wield it however they desire. If this were true, I would be very concerned! Claiming humans have God-like autonomy is highly dangerous and is not biblical. What the Bible does say is that God's power manifests through vessels of weakness (2 Corinthians 12:9) who are *under authority* (Matthew 8:8–10), not through special people with special powers. Peter, Paul, and the early disciples were not superheroes; they were human beings, emptied of self, crucified with Christ (Galatians 2:20), and filled with the Spirit of God. What I am getting at is that kenotic Christology fundamentally promotes humility, not God-like autonomy. Jesus demonstrated a life of power through surrender. Kenotic Christology is the foundation that supports a yielded life. It tells us that the pathway to purity and power lies in self-emptying and dependence upon God. It explains that His desire is that we be holy as He is Holy and that we live a life marked by miraculous power. The way this happens is through living radical, minute-by-minute surrender to the lordship of Jesus Christ. This is a core gospel message: you die to the flesh to live in resurrection power.

At the end of His earthly ministry, most likely in the Garden of Gethsemane, Jesus gave his last teaching to His disciples. Jesus employed a metaphor that mirrored His relationship with the Father, calling His followers into relationship with Himself. He told them, "I am the vine, you are the branches; he who abides in Me and I in him, he bears much fruit, for apart from Me you can do *nothing*" (John 15:5).

I am hoping this theme sounds familiar by now! When Jesus says "nothing," he means *nothing!* He is telling His disciples that the dependence and self-surrender He modeled are now the very things He is calling us to embody. Jesus could do nothing apart from the Father, but through His life of yielded abiding in God, He bore much fruit and represented the Father to the world. Now, Jesus is telling His followers they can do nothing apart from Him, but through lives of yielded abiding, they will bear much fruit and represent Jesus to the world. This is amazing!

We are created to function from union with Christ. This union is realized through the third member of the Trinity, the Holy Spirit. Jesus tells us that it is better for Him to go to the Father because He will send us the Holy Spirit (John 14:15–31). Jesus was one person, but His plan was to make a way for all of humanity to now enter into the dynamic place of union through the Holy Spirit. He came to multiply His life billions of times over, living and expressing Himself through the Holy Spirit in each one of us! This is how the Body of Christ comes to life! We each, through union with the Holy Spirit, begin to express different aspects of Jesus's nature and together become a living incarnation of Christ.

This union is established and maintained through a life of prayer. Heidi Baker, a missionary being used to transform the nation of Mozambique, often preaches that "All fruitfulness flows from intimacy with Jesus."[6] Her words marked me as a young man serving her ministry in Africa and have influenced my spiritual walk ever since. Without Jesus, we can do nothing, but in Him, we can do all things. Prayer is where we learn what being "in Him" is all about.

Before God began breaking my pride and willfulness, I thought living the Christian life was up to me to do in my own strength. At my lowest, my eyes were opened to understand Jesus's statement "You can do nothing apart from me" in a whole new light. I was forced to recognize that the fruit of my striving was bad and therefore I had to reconfigure how to go about life. I began to recognize that prayer is paramount to healthy spirituality. It is not a suggestion but an imperative. I was eager to learn how to pray and get after it, but I found this was not as easy as I had hoped. There were many glass ceilings that I had to break through before I could enter into the heart of prayer.

Many in the church are lacking understanding of how to pray. This is because prayer is trapped in a religious box that has served to suck the life, passion, and vigor out of this glorious gift. Imagine you received a letter in the mail tomorrow inviting you to spend the day with Billy Graham. The letter reads that he desires a conversation with you. My guess is that no matter your schedule, you would jump at the occasion, dropping all your plans to get on a plane to fly to make the appointment. It would be an incredible honor. God far surpasses Billy in both wisdom and power, and He desires to speak with you. In fact, He continuously makes Himself available to engage with you personally. Prayer is the most extraordinary opportunity imaginable. When I say it is locked in a religious box, I am speaking to the reality that we have lost the wonder of what we are doing. So many express the sentiment that they *should* be praying more. Others are pleased with themselves when they check the box that they concentrated really hard for a ten-minute devotional time. This falls so short of what prayer is intended to be.

Prayer is more than speaking to God verbally—it can be danced, sung, wept, sighed, and acted out. In my experience, the most impactful and transformative times of prayer I have had with the Father have been when I express the unction within me through creative expression. We cannot underestimate the power of this expression. David danced, Jesus wept, and Isaiah lay on his side; there is no formula or demand to this, only permission granted. We are allowed freedom to use creativity in expressing ourselves to God. The truth is that our actions often speak louder than our words. Nonverbal communication gives deeper meaning to the words that we speak. The reason we kneel in prayer or raise our hands in praise is because prayer is a holistic experience, encompassing spirit, soul, and body. Prayer should consume the whole person, as every facet of our being was designed for communion with God. This begins in the secret place, as His kingdom is inside out. Every creation is conceived first in the imagination. Learning to abide in prayer allows God access to this sacred real estate within. Our minds become fertile soil in which He can plant His mustard-seed promises.

When we understand this is our goal, our natural tendency is to try to make it happen in our own energy or attempt to convince God to act through our prayers. In truth, He desires to work through us, but He can only do so when we are in a posture of receptivity. One of the biggest problems I consistently meet in those I lead is a lack of ability to connect with God in prayer. I've heard the question, "What do I do?" or "What do I say?" many times. I've learned that this is the talk of spiritual infants, which is not a bad thing! I know this because I used to be one. In the natural realm, we are born infants and, through nourishment, experience ongoing development into maturity; it is no different in the spiritual realm. God doesn't despise our immaturity, because He delights in parenting us. It's His job! He is gracious to nourish us with spiritual milk and continually raise us up into His likeness (1 Peter 2:2). These questions demonstrate immaturity because they are focused on self rather than God. The initial emphasis in prayer should not be on what we have to offer, but rather on what God desires to give.

Prevenient grace is a core doctrine of the church. It teaches that God pursued us, even while we were sinners, and we responded to His invitation. Salvation did not take place because we found God, but because God came and pursued us. This doctrine is important and absolutely true, but to be honest, it used to mean nothing to me! I had it in my mind that prevenient grace only applied to an evening in 1995 when I accepted Jesus into my heart as a little boy and got saved. I've now come to recognize that prevenient grace does not apply only to our first day in Christ, but to all of them! We love because He first loves us, every single day (1 John 4:19). His mercies are new every morning (Lamentations 3:22–23). This has significant repercussions on what prayer should look like. Our first priority in prayer is not what to do, but how to receive the prevenient, relentless love of our Father.

In Psalm 131, David beautifully captures the posture of receiving. He prays, "Surely I have composed and quieted my soul; like a child rests against his mother, so my soul is like a weaned child within me" (Psalm 131:2). I specifically want to key in on the words *quiet* and *rest,* as these serve as my entry points into prayer. A soul that is stilled is prepared to receive from God. What this looks like for me is something called *resting prayer.* Envision a sponge being cast into the midst of the sea; all it can do is rest and soak up water. In this analogy, I am the sponge, and the sea is God's vast love. I begin most days by putting on worship music, getting a pillow on the ground, and lying face-down before the Lord. I don't work or strive or try to do anything. In fact, it is quite the opposite. I strive to do nothing and enter into the rest of God (Hebrews 4:11).

I will be honest and disclose that the first years that I began doing this, I would often feel guilty. I am hardwired as an achiever, so spending excess amounts of time in a childlike posture of receiving was really uncomfortable. I struggled, wondering if I was being lazy. As I began in ministry, I was surprised as these feelings only intensified. I would struggle with thoughts such as, "How many people have you met with?" and "What results is this accomplishing?" I share this because I know this relates to anyone in any profession. There are always a million things on our "to-do" lists screaming for our attention! I've come to now recognize that this is an attack of hell to try to quench our thirst for prayer. The uncomfortable truth is that the enemy will do anything to keep us from praying, including getting us busy doing good, Christian things. Intentionally carving out time to do nothing but receive the Love of the Father is the most faith-filled thing you can do with your time each day.

I continued battling my feelings of guilt over "wasting" time in prayer for a number of years. I use the word *waste* because that is often what this time feels like. In truth, lavishing time on Jesus extravagantly is impractical and extremely wasteful. It is no different from when Mary poured out the whole bottle of perfume at the feet of Jesus; it makes no sense to the carnal mind. We must remember that no matter how unproductive prayer may appear, it is endlessly beautiful to God. The reality with prayer is that some days it feels amazing and some days it feels very bland. Regardless of what I feel, I have learned to yield to Jesus and trust that He is with me, no matter my emotional state. I'll never forget the moment when this lesson finally hit home and the feelings of guilt and laziness were broken off of my life.

I had just finished a four-month internship at a church, and I was getting ready to do overseas missions for a few months. I had struggled most of the four months with the constant nagging guilt of wondering whether I was lazy because I was praying too much while all the other staff members seemed to be much more productive than me. I had prioritized resting prayer faithfully and fought for connection with Jesus even through the dryness I often experienced. (People have asked me what it looks like practically to fight for connection when you feel a block in prayer. For me, most often it's through journaling. I seek to gain understanding of wandering thoughts, negative emotions, apathy, etc. I process what I am experiencing as vulnerably as I can with God. I find He is always present with my authentic self.) On my last day of the internship before I flew out, I ran into one of the staff members at a coffee shop, and we began chatting. At one point, he looked at me and said, "I've been thinking about this a lot today. You've been here four months, and I've been on staff for four years. I confessed to God this afternoon that in my estimation, He accomplished more through you in these months than He has through me these last years. I've watched you, and all you've done is pray. I think there is something to that." He went on to describe how he was challenged to re-prioritize prayer in his life and ministry as he had witnessed the momentum of God rest upon the few ministry opportunities I had engaged in. His words sank deep into me and finally liberated me from the guilt! God's inside-out method was actually working, and I was bearing fruit!

Time is extremely valuable, and how we invest it reveals what is most important to us. Where our treasure is, our hearts will lie (Matthew 6:21). Investing time in the secret place demonstrates to Jesus that He is our treasure. This also means that prayerlessness communicates the opposite. It sends a clear-cut message that Jesus is not the Pearl of Great Price in our eyes. We must consistently join Mary in choosing the better portion of sitting at the Lord's feet (Luke 10:39) and recognize that in the end, we will never regret a moment spent being intimate with Jesus. No matter how much we have going on, we are too busy not to pray. Martin Luther is quoted as saying, "I have so much to do today that I'm going to need to spend three hours in prayer in order to be able to get it all done." This is kingdom-logic and not the wisdom of the world, but it works!

It has been a marvel for me to experience, but I can testify that it is during this time of resting in the love of God that the vast majority of the decisions I make in leadership originate. As I lie before the feet of Jesus, doing my best to focus my heart and affections upon Him, many thoughts begin to pop into my mind. I used to think this was mental wandering and inherently bad, but over time, I discovered this most often is the Spirit of God gifting me with ideas and strategy for my day. Countless times, He will bring someone to mind, show me a conversation I need to have, or give me direction for a decision that is looming. As I have described, I am not praying anything during this time; I am simply receiving! I have had individuals approach me over creative ideas I've implemented in leadership and ask me, "Where did you get that idea? It is seriously brilliant!" I smile and tell them it popped into my mind as I was resting in the love of God. It honestly is that simple. I cannot even begin to describe to you the fruitfulness that has resulted from these ideas!

In private prayer, there are two voices involved: our own and God's. In this equation, only one of those voices formed the galaxies. (It is a marvel to me that we put so much emphasis on what we are to say!) We must prioritize His voice first and spend time resting and listening (Isaiah 55:2). I was convicted of this in college when I realized that I would effortlessly spend three hours waiting in line for a roller coaster, yet struggled to wait on His voice for ten minutes. As I pondered this, I recognized the significance that patience plays in prayer. Waiting on the Lord is not a passive experience but an act of absolute focus. Similar to a hunter who camps in a blind for countless hours in hopes of large game passing by, in prayer it is required we take the same posture. This can seem counterintuitive at first glance because the external posture of resting is one of laziness. This is true, but it is a huge mistake to think this is easy!

Jeanne Guyon, in her book titled *Experiencing the Depths of Jesus Christ,* writes, "The main element of the soul is the *will,* and the soul must *will* to become neutral and passive, waiting entirely upon God. Can you not see that this condition of utter passivity, this state of doing nothing and waiting upon God, is actually the highest activity of the will? Listen to your soul as it says, 'I am *willing* with all the power of my being that the desire of God be accomplished within me. I am *willing* to be here, ceasing from all my activity and all of my power, so that God might have His desire of fully possessing me.'"[7]

In other words, though this is a posture of external laziness, internally this is a discipline cultivated through countless hours and many years invested seeking the Face of God. In practical terms, this looks like setting your intention upon Jesus—focusing your thoughts, imagination, and affection upon Him. This requires a persistent turning back to Him over and over as your heart wonders. This is invaluable. It is where you find your emotional equilibrium and peace for each day.

Prayer begins in this way, learning to wait and receive the love of God, but it does not end there. God is desiring conversation. The ultimate goal of New Testament prayer is not to pray to God, but *with Him*. Praying to God makes it sound like we are writing a letter and sending it to Him. There is no expectation of an immediate reply when you send things by mail. When you are sitting with a friend over coffee, it's a much different dynamic. The conversation ebbs and flows as two people share time and space together. This is what praying with God looks like. It is a dialogue between two good friends (John 15:15).

Prayer is itself an act of co-laboring. Though God's voice should be prioritized, He has called us to express ourselves in this relationship. Once we have made ourselves available to His prevenient grace and received of His love, we are then prepared to express ourselves in anointed prayer. I like thinking of prayer as art. Creativity is woven into it at every level. Similarly to how a painter first seeks inspiration before making any strokes with the brush, in times of resting prayer, we are finding inspiration before expressing ourselves to God. Ecclesiastes 5:2 exhorts us, "Do not be hasty in word or impulsive in thought to bring up a matter in the Presence of God." We must approach prayer like an artist approaches a blank canvas. We aren't coming to spew whatever comes to mind but to express ourselves in raw and beautiful authenticity to Jesus. Do not mistake this for a paradigm of perfection and performance. God is not an art critic. He is like a parent that loves anything His children make, not because it looks like Van Gogh's *Starry Night,* but because they passionately put their hearts into it. It's passion that makes prayer beautiful.

I've heard the question, "Why do I need to pray if God already knows what I am going to say?" This is a question that is asked when viewing prayer as scientific and formulaic. This gets us in trouble because prayer is art! We must recognize how much God values creativity.

Envision this scenario: A wife goes grocery shopping and stocks the refrigerator with all kinds of wonderful ingredients. She unloads the groceries and then takes off to go the gym before her husband and kids come home and expect dinner. An hour and a half later, she walks through the front door to the smell of many beautiful aromas flooding from the kitchen. She turns the corner to see her husband and kids at work preparing dinner, and the table is perfectly set. They have turned the ingredients she purchased into a meal! She is overwhelmed with joy at this surprise blessing. It makes no difference to her that she was the one who had stocked the refrigerator because the dinner prepared was something much greater than the sum total of all the ingredients purchased. Human creativity and love were the added elements that brought the groceries to life! Prayer is no different.

When we spend time resting in the love of God, we receive the anointing of heaven. He deposits His inspiration into our hearts and minds. He weaves the passion of His heart into ours, or in other words, God stocks the refrigerator with the groceries! We become "stocked" whenever we receive the love of God. Once this filling takes place, we are equipped to take the raw material of His inspiration and express it through our unique personalities in love to Him. This absolutely thrills His heart! When we pray with passion, sowing our hearts into the act, we create a kingdom artifact that He keeps right in front of Him. Revelation describes our prayers as a bowl of burning incense that sits before the throne of God (Revelation 5:8). The Father adores our prayers!

As I began spending more and more hours in prayer with God, I found His inspiration within leading me into passionate expression of love toward Jesus. I call this adoration. Very quickly, I realized that to express this passion to Jesus, something else was necessitated. The truth is, passion never travels alone; it always is accompanied by vulnerability. Vulnerability intimidated me while I was growing up. This is because I am an introvert and my mother is one of the most social and vulnerable people I have ever met. I used to be terrified of being in public places with her because I never knew what she was going to do, or share, or even worse, ask me to share in front of people that were as good as strangers to me! I have countless memories where she made me feel extremely uncomfortable. What I began to discover is that my discomfort toward vulnerability became a source of hindrance to my prayer life. I began to recognize the presence of passion within my heart, and yet an inability to express it because I was terrified of exposing myself so openly.

Though my mom often embarrassed me in public because of her passion and vulnerability, one of the greatest gifts she gave me in her parenting was that she always pursued my heart. What I mean by this is she would sit with me (sometimes for hours) when I was hurting and ask me questions, attempting to get me to share about my emotions. She was teaching me about the beauty of vulnerability and ultimately demonstrating to my young and tender heart how to cultivate intimacy. I never recognized the beauty of what she was teaching me until I began to pursue God in prayer.

As I began seeking Him fervently, in a strangely familiar way, God began to pursue my heart much like my mother did. As I would sit with the Lord, I would sense His Spirit ever so gently drawing me into vulnerability. In a very strange way, this would trigger deep discomfort and make me feel loved at the same time. This was by no means an overnight process, as I was a very shut off from my emotions, but as time progressed, His softening became tangible.

I remember the first time I felt the Holy Spirit prompting me to sing to the Lord. I was alone in a prayer chapel and felt a nearly uncontrollable desire to sing. I had never sung in my life. I used to stand silent at church during worship, as I made no connection to the songs being played. My mother used to nudge me and tell me to sing, and I would mockingly sing operatically and laugh. I had no idea what it meant to sing to the Lord.

In the chapel that night, I could feel words within me that seemed as though they were going to burst forth from my mouth. I didn't know what to do and was scared to death, yet I found the urge impossible to resist, and so I began to sing. It was awkward and jumbled, but I felt my heart come alive. Over the following months, I began doing it more and more. I would spontaneously sing my heart out to Jesus. In the beginning, it made me feel extremely vulnerable, childlike, and even silly, but I experienced His grace. I was learning the art of prayer.

The next step in this progression was much more difficult for me. When I tell you that I didn't sing, it's true. When I tell you I didn't dance, it's an absolute. I was again in a prayer chapel, seeking the Lord, when suddenly an urge to dance rose up within me. I felt the Lord tell me, "I want you to dance before Me." I don't have words to describe how uncomfortable this made me feel. I was squeamish. In spite of my feelings, all I could think in the moment was that David danced in his underwear, and if I desired to be a man after God's heart, I too could not be afraid of being undignified. So I did it, sort of. I doubt the movements my body made qualify as dance, or art of any kind, but I expressed my heart physically to God and experienced His grace. I honestly felt like I was naked. I can't imagine feeling more exposed than I did that evening, but I knew it was good. God continued drawing me deeper and deeper into vulnerability. I still do not consider myself a dancer, but I have since had moments of raw expression where I've danced before Him with all my might. Truthfully, it's uncomfortable writing this for anyone to read, but I do it because I believe it's important to cast vision for what passion in prayer can actually look like.

Acts 13:2 tells us the leaders of the church in Antioch were "ministering unto the Lord." During this time of vertical ministry "unto the Lord," God spoke and birthed one of the most successful missionary ventures in the history of the church. The principle is that vertical ministry should always come before horizontal ministry. This is how God in His wisdom ordained it. Fruitful branches are the ones connected to the vine- adoration precedes intercession.

Singing and dancing before the Lord helped me receive His grace and connect to His heart. This was my process of learning to fulfill my ministry unto the Lord. I began to find that as I grew in connection to God, it became much easier to discern His voice. This positioned me to begin interceding with God and not just to Him. As I "wasted" time worshipping Him, Jesus began to disclose himself to me. This often came, and still comes, in the form of sharing the burdens He carries for those He has entrusted to my leadership.

Jesus lives to make intercession for His Bride, so you can rest assured knowing He is always praying for us (Hebrews 7:25)! *Intercession* literally means to "stand in the gap" for others and pray the will of God for their lives. We are most effective in this when the prayers of His heart become the prayers of ours. You can have great faith that a prayer will be answered when you know it is something that He is praying too! When our prayers and His become one, there is agreement between heaven and earth. This is what co-laboring with God to see His kingdom come looks like, and it can only happen when you are praying with Him!

In intercessory prayer, perspective makes all the difference. Our vantage point greatly dictates how and what we pray. A story is recorded in 2 Kings, chapter 6, about the prophet Elisha and his servant. The city they are in gets surrounded by an army seeking to kill Elisha. The servant looks out and is in distress. In response, Elisha calmly prays that the Lord will open the servant's eyes to see what is really taking place. The servant looks out and sees that Elisha is surrounded by chariots of fire. There was nothing to fear; God was with Elisha, and he was aware of it!

I've found that in intercessory prayer we have an important choice to make. We either identify with the servant or with the prophet. When we pray as the servant, we will begin pleading with God, begging for salvation, escape, or things of this nature. This is what it looks like to pray from an earthly perspective. When we pray as the prophet, we are praying with God—aware of His activity—confident that no matter how big the problem or severe the negativity we are facing, God is for us and no one can stand against us (Romans 8:31).

A number of years, ago my mom was going through a very difficult season and was experiencing severe sickness. It was horrible for her and horrible to feel helpless as she suffered. I remember one night we were on a phone call, and I was praying for her. I found that all my prayers were essentially the same. I was begging and pleading with God to heal my mom. In the middle of the prayer, I intuitively recognized something was wrong with this and stopped praying abruptly. I realized I never stopped to listen to what God wanted to speak or consulted Him for how to pray. I was experiencing negative emotions because my mom was suffering and jumped straight into intercession. This was highly ineffective because I wasn't praying with God, I was being led my own emotions, praying what I thought was best, with the assumption that my prayer was the same as His. As I realized I was doing this, I ceased begging, did my best to quiet my mind and ask the Lord how to pray for my mom, and then did according to what I discerned. A few minutes later, we hung up the phone, and I was disturbed. I recognized that I still knew very little about the nature of prayer and that I had developed a pattern of hastily praying out of my emotion rather than connection.

We are still in the process of seeing my mother's health restored. Over the last years, there has been progress, but we have still not seen full healing. I share this because I don't want you to think this is a magic formula. God is not a genie in a bottle but a person we are learning to pray with. I desire the Holy Spirit to feel very comfortable in my presence. I want Him to be very free to do what He wants, and also to never feel pressured by me to do something He doesn't. This tension is something I am continually learning to navigate in regard to intercessory prayer. God does not always work the way we want Him to. His agenda is often very different from what ours is. We have a tendency to want immediate results, and sometimes God works this way, answering our prayers in an instant. Other times, it is His delight to work over a decade. We don't get to decide this, and regardless of His methods, our job is to listen and obey. It is important to recognize that intercession is not a one-time event but a discipline that requires endurance. Persevering prayer is often required before we see a breakthrough (Luke 18:1–8). This is not because we are changing God's mind, but because persevering through disappointment changes us. We get emptied of our own agendas in this process, which positions us to be conduits of His agenda breaking into earth through our prayers.

In October of 2017, the Lord put a burden on my heart to begin praying for prodigals to come home to our church family. I had heard testimonies from a pastor in Dallas whose church had seen many hurt by religiosity restored into relationship with the Father, and I was stirred. I was at our weekly Tuesday morning prayer meeting, and God began speaking to me about His lost sheep. As a church, we began crying out for the prodigal sons and daughters to come back to the Father. We prayed that embittered hearts would sense a strange desire to go to church and that God would literally draw them to us. I knew we were praying with God and partnering with His agenda.

Remarkably, within ten days, I had a young man approach me at the altar post-service, tears streaming down his face, confessing to me that he'd been wounded by a church four years prior and had run far from God. He made sure I knew how crazy it was that he was in church and especially that he would even talk with a pastor. I was almost in shock. I was talking to a prodigal son who was weeping under conviction of God's mighty love, and he was experiencing the Father's embrace! It didn't stop there. Within two months, I had seven different individuals personally testify to me of this same thing. One of these was a person the Lord gave me a burden to specifically pray for. Through a series of events, he ended up coming to church and after service told me, "It's strange, but I know something is drawing me here." It is incredible how powerful our prayers are when we partner with God in intercession!

God's kingdom is inside out. The fulfillment of the mandate to create heaven on earth begins within. In God's wisdom, He first instructs those He has called to change the world through to invest time and passion into a small, hidden place of confinement called the prayer closet. This makes no sense from a worldly perspective, but we are not trying to create the kingdom of this world! It is still a divine mystery to me on how it happens, but somehow the investment into this small, enclosed space is what leads to a life of endless opportunity. The kingdom of God truly is like a peck of leaven that gets hidden in the dough. It is at first invisible to the naked eye and yet suddenly causes the whole lump to rise (Matthew 13:33). Anointed times of prayer are where God begins to leaven our hearts with His dreams and desires for our lives. These start small and hidden, but they don't stay that way! (For additional resources to journey deeper into the art of prayer, see endnotes.[8])

CHAPTER SIX

Servants and Sons

*No longer do I call you slaves, for the slave does not know
what the master is doing: but I have called you friends.*

———

JOHN 15:15

T HE TIME I SPENT IN THE PRAYER CLOSET BEGAN TO TRANSLATE TO
fruitfulness in my life. After years spent seeking Him in
hiddenness, I very suddenly found myself in situations where I was
ministering to people and seeing them experience God through my
words and actions. This was an adjustment for me. I didn't know
how, but the leaven of the kingdom was on the rise in me. During the
years of hiddenness, God had revealed His desire for my life: I was
called to the Bride of Christ—the church. This was the last thing

I had ever considered becoming, but I knew pastoral ministry was my God-given calling. He put a passion for revival in my heart and a dream to create a church environment so dynamic in nature that it empowered people to go out and fulfill their God-given dreams. Before I knew it, I was a twenty-two-year-old on staff at a church and positioned to start seeing this desire come to fruition. For me, this meant it was time to learn how to translate the lessons learned in the secret place to the real world.

The next three years were a real-life classroom, and instructional content came in the form of mistakes made. The Lord had to recalibrate me into learning how to live His way. In the last section of the book, I mentioned that the wildness in me died on that day with my face in the sand. The fear of the Lord consumed me and took its place. This did not mean that I walked in perfect obedience, but that I desired to! I began to recognize that the behaviors that had "worked" in trying to fulfill my own dreams and ambitions were unacceptable when trying to create something with God. His ways are very different from ours (Isaiah 55:8–9), and as we are junior partners in the family business of building the kingdom, it's His way or the highway!

When the Lord broke me, I was forced to confront how manipulative my actions had been and, at the same time, face the fact that I had been trying to convince God to endorse this behavior. On the other side of the breaking, I wanted nothing to do with this behavior. I found a holy fear of the Lord present within me, which manifested as a sincere distaste toward trying to make something happen in my own power. My desire became to do His will—I lost the strength and energy necessary to strive my way into achievement. My aim became to be a wholly submitted servant of Jesus. My great joy became helping Him accomplish what He is already at work doing. In this, I found there is so much momentum in His endeavors because He is the life-force of all creation. There is no striving necessary. In His presence, there is access to the joy of heaven that strengthens and empowers us to accomplish more than we thought possible. I am in no way advocating laziness; there is much work to do! I am simply distinguishing between the drain of tirelessly striving to manufacture a fulfilling life and the inspired, supernatural effectiveness that comes from laboring with God.

Which course we take in this boils down to how we decide to use the gift of the human will we've each been given. Our will is the decision-making faculty inside our souls. Decision-making is one of the most constant and crucial dilemmas we face in life. We are bombarded with decisions ranging from miniscule to major every single day. How we make decisions is a window that reveals the quality of our relationship with Jesus. It is a litmus test that discloses our level of surrender. Throughout this book, I have already detailed how independence derails our decision-making, alienating us from the wisdom of heaven in exchange for reliance upon the power of human rationale. This has led to the creation of a sin-diseased planet. God came to liberate us from operating in this paradigm by sanctifying us and bringing us into joyful submission to the lordship of Jesus Christ. In other words, He makes us faithful servants. This is incredible—however, the picture is incomplete. Servanthood is not God's utmost desire for our lives—He calls us to something greater!

In John 15:15, after three years of the disciples following Jesus, He tells them, "No longer do I call you slaves, for the slave does not know what his master is doing, but I have called you friends, for all things that I have heard from My Father I have made known to you."

Jesus tells us that servants (slaves) don't know what the Master is doing. If you think about the analogy, it makes sense. Servants don't ask questions or even have conversations with their master; they simply do what they are told. The highest form of servanthood is perfect obedience—this is what it looks like for servants to master their craft.

During my junior year of high school, I made unethical decisions in regard to my academic performance. Yes, I mean I cheated. The most heinous offense was in an upper division science class that also was accredited through a local university. Through some immoral means, a person in the class obtained the answers to the end-of-the-year final exam. I decided that rather than studying, I would simply fill out the test with the answers I'd been given and intentionally mark a few responses as incorrect to cover my tracks. The worst part of this story is that this breach of integrity hardly bothered me. The next year, I graduated and moved to another state to attend university. It was during this time that God began dealing with me.

One night, during my sophomore year of university, I was up late praying in a chapel, and the Lord spoke clearly to me. He told me, "You need to go back to your chemistry teacher and repent for how you took advantage of her and tell her what you did." This came out of left field, and I was shocked. I wish I could say that in this moment I demonstrated the heart of a faithful, obedient servant of Christ Jesus and joyfully agreed, but I would be lying. Instead, I said to myself, "That is just guilt trying to haunt me. I've been forgiven of that." With those words, I justified my dismissal of the Lord's command and went on with my day. No more than two weeks later, I was home visiting my family during a break from university. I'd been wanting a new pair of running shoes, and so I went with my family to the shoe store. I was sitting on a bench, trying on a new pair of sweet shoes, and I heard a voice ring out, "Jordan Verner!"

Instantly, I whipped my head around and to my dismay, I saw the smiling face of my sweet chemistry teacher. I did my best to keep a facade that hid my shame, but I couldn't hide it from myself. We talked for a few minutes, and all I can remember is I could barely concentrate because my heart was beating so fast. We eventually said our casual goodbyes and "nice to see yous," but the intense conviction would not leave me. The Lord then asked me, "Are you ready to obey me now?"

I still wasn't ready, at least not in that moment, and so I crept out of the store unnoticed. Quick obedience always makes things easier in the long run because it saves you from the agony of waiting. The next two days, all I could think about was what I knew I had to do. The following Monday came, and I very sheepishly marched the halls of my old high school at lunch break. I made my way to the chemistry lab, found my teacher, and asked if I could speak to her privately. I obeyed the Lord and repented of my sin, and with tears in her eyes, she forgave me. I left feeling vulnerable but aware of God's pleasure over me—I was slowly surrendering my will to the lordship of Jesus and learning what servanthood consisted of. We are all servants of Christ and will be growing in this office for the rest of our lives.

There are still, constantly, areas of my life where I am learning to be obedient. In recent years, my biggest area of growth has been obeying Jesus in the small, ordinary instructions He gives me. Many times, I have disregarded small promptings such as "Buy the lunch of the person who is behind you in line," or "Text so-and-so," or "Go to that event." For this reason, I don't foresee my growth curve stopping anytime soon.

Servanthood is the foundation that friendship rests upon. Building your life upon obedience and submission to the lordship of Jesus Christ is what positions you to enter into the promotion of friendship with God. I use the word *promotion* because friendship with God entails a quality of relationship that far exceeds what a servant could ever hope for. Friends converse and discuss decisions together. Friends disclose hidden hopes and disappointments. In the same way, Jesus made all things known to His disciples, and they became his friends.

When operating in pride and independence, we make decisions apart from the Father. On the contrary, as broken, submitted servants we make decisions out of obedience. Though this posture of submission is really good, it is incomplete. The truth is that there are many decisions we face where God does not directly tell us what to do. As faithful servants, we bring the situation before Him and ask for guidance, but what happens when we wait and seek in prayer, but no answer comes? I used to panic when this happened. However, I've learned that this scenario is an invitation into friendship. I've learned to interpret God's silence in this context as an indicator that He trusts me to make the decision myself. Though this sounds like a relapse into an independence paradigm, I assure you it is far from this.

When my brother Riley and I were kids, we used to love getting ice cream from the ice cream truck that used to circle through our neighborhood playing loud music. I have countless memories of trying to scrape the house for spare change in time to catch the truck before it was too late.

One particular afternoon, my mom and brother were home when the obnoxious music began ringing from outside the house. My brother began his hunt for a dollar and fifty cents. He asked my mom, who was reading a book, for money and was told that if he wanted an ice cream, he'd have to find the money himself. A couple minutes later, he confidently emerged with a couple bucks and joyfully made for the front door. On his was out, he yelled to my mom, "Do you want one?"

She replied, "Yes, if you have enough, get me a rocket pop!"

Five minutes later, Riley returned with a rocket pop for my mom. She was immersed in her book and so took the ice cream with gratitude and kept reading. A few moments passed, and she looked up from her book at my brother, who was now sitting across the room from her with a smile on his face, and noticed he didn't have any ice cream. She asked him, "Where is your ice cream?"

"I only had enough for one," Riley disclosed with a grin.

"And you got one for me?" my mom exclaimed. My mom was so blessed that she immediately threw the book down, got her purse, and gave my brother a five-dollar bill, telling him to go and get whatever he wanted! Riley's decision compelled my mom into action.

Let me unpack this: If my mom had called out to my brother on his way out the door, "Use that dollar and fifty cents and get me an ice cream cone instead!" he would have been faced with a difficult choice of obedience. This is what servanthood consists of. We will face these situations throughout our lives, and the aim is to always, unconditionally say yes, no matter how much it hurts.

What makes this story so precious is that he chose to get my mom the ice cream cone of his own accord. He used the freedom he was given to choose love, and it moved my mother's heart deeply. In the same way, I've discovered God often remains silent in order to create opportunity for my heart to be revealed. My brother made the decision of how to use his spare change with my mom in mind—this is what friendship is all about. I deeply desire to live my life and make decisions always with the Father in mind, using freedom as an opportunity to demonstrate my love for Him (2 Corinthians 3:17–18). In servanthood, we are locked into a binary decision-making process; it's either "Yes, I will obey" or "No, I will not." In friendship, endless creativity can be used because the world is our canvas. We can endlessly imagine and create with love as our inspiration.

After the pride in my life was exposed, I became very comfortable living as a servant. I disclosed earlier that I was terrified of "making something happen." In this place, the Lord began bringing me to divergent paths of life where I had to start making some very big decisions (or at least, they felt that way at the time!). I wanted to be a faithful servant, and so I would tell God, "Tell me what to do, Lord, and I will obey." I would then hear nothing but crickets. This distressed me greatly. I would scrutinize and anguish over the decisions and try to figure out what I had done wrong to constitute God not speaking to me. I had no concept of what friendship with God looked like.

I still remember the day when the Lord opened my eyes to the dynamic at play. He whispered to me, "What do you want to do?"

I instinctively quipped back, "Whatever you want me to, Lord!"

He persisted, "But what do you want to do?" His question settled into my spirit, and my mind began to churn. He began to reveal to me deeper understanding of the relationship He desired to have with me. The analogy that came to my mind was a son trained in the Father's business who finally has "graduated" to the point of going on a business trip by himself. The Father entrusts the son with His authority, denoting that the young man is able to make decisions on behalf of the Father. This is the ultimate seal of approval—the son is trusted by the Father. As I pondered this, God began to minister to my heart. I knew why He was asking me "What do you want to do?" He was communicating His approval and trust of my heart. We were becoming friends.

It's been years since this revelation came to me, and I have since made many life-altering decisions as God's friend. To reiterate once more, I will never cease seeking to grow in servanthood, becoming completely obedient to Lord Jesus. Yet when He entrusts me with a decision, it is my aim to use the liberty I have received to demonstrate my love for Him. I seek to express myself in faith of who He is. Consequently, these crucial decisions have together served as a launchpad for kingdom creativity through my life.

I pastor a church called River House, which I planted in 2016 and which has seen much kingdom fruitfulness. I have confessed to our church family that God never told me to plant River House. I actually brought the idea to Him, many times. There were multiple instances where He said no and there was no grace attached to the idea. In fact, less than six months before the church started, He had told me to surrender the thought and shelve it. Due to the nature of the circumstances I was in, I thought this meant for a minimum of five years. Through this, He was growing me as a servant in obedience. A few months later, after an extended period of fasting, I felt Him put the decision back on my lap. I knew He was giving me permission to decide what I wanted, and I chose to risk. I've heard it said that faith is spelled R-I-S-K. In my opinion, the people of God should be the most faith-filled, entrepreneurial, risk-taking individuals on the planet! We are following the God who calls us to see the invisible and do the impossible; risk is involved at every turn of life with Jesus! I will share more about River House in a later chapter detailing what God has done in the wake of this risk. For now, it suffices to tell you that God was with me in this leap of faith.

It is imperative that we, as children of God, come to understand the permission we have been given in Christ Jesus. If we fail to recognize God's invitation into friendship, we become vulnerable to red-light Christianity. This term refers to a paradigm where we are stagnant until God tells us to do something directly. This happens when we relate to God *only* as servants. The truth is that we have been given a green light in Christ! Jesus tells to "*Go* and make disciples of all nations, baptizing them in the name of the Father and of the Son and of the Holy Spirit" (Matthew 28:19). Permission has been granted, and we are allowed to bring ideas to Him. We are junior partners in the family business, and He loves to hear them!

Amazingly enough, sometimes He actually gets behind them! We have been told to "Go!"—to risk, to step out in faith and know that God is with us!

Everything I am speaking of flows from a humble heart and dependent relationship with Jesus. Above all else, humility is the key to operating in a co-laboring relationship with Jesus. It is the heart of true servanthood and the garden bed in which friendship with God can grow. Humility precedes trust. Without it, we remain bound in the binary decision-making paradigm of obedient servanthood, which falls so far short of God's fullness for our lives. God is committed to exposing and breaking pride so that we can be entrusted to live from a place of friendship with Him.

First Peter 5:5 says, "God opposes the proud but gives grace to the humble." The word *grace* is *charis*, which is also translated as *favor* in other New Testament passages. Luke 2:52 tells us that the young boy, Jesus, grew in *charis* with both God and man. This is a fascinating verse. If Jesus grew in favor with God, it is safe to say that we need to do the same! I realize now that as I demonstrated humility in obedience to God, He began entrusting more decisions to me in friendship. Over the past few years, I've compiled a track record of wise, fruitful decisions, and something incredible started to happen—favor began to increase!

CHAPTER SEVEN

Increasing in Favor

And Jesus increased in wisdom and in stature
and in favor with God and man.

———

LUKE 2:52

UNDERSTANDING OUR IDENTITY AS SONS AND DAUGHTERS IS foundational to our understanding of divine favor. God's love and acceptance of us are not based on our performance; they are based on His knowledge of who we really are. He ransomed us from our sin and brokenness, placing our shame on Jesus, and gave us favor instead. Through the cross of Calvary, God made a way for humanity to become a new creation in Christ. "In Christ" means that once we have become born-again, our life, identity, and inheritance are located within the person of Jesus Christ. It is impossible for the Father to look at us and not see Jesus. "In Christ" is the most highly favored place in all the created order. Whenever God looks upon Jesus, He smiles as He sees His beloved son in whom He is well pleased! We live within the Beloved One; this means that God looks at us and smiles because we are in Christ! We are accepted, loved, and smiled upon (also known as favored) by God.

Favor was something that I lacked understanding of until four years ago. Up until that point, I would have described favor as a type of spiritual luck that I really hoped to have. I certainly wanted favor on my life and could easily recognize people who had been given it, but I didn't have language to define it, so it remained a mystery. Four years ago, someone prayed over me that God would open my eyes to the favor God had given me, and those words stuck. In response to this, I began seeking to understand the nature of divine favor. As I share my process of discovery, my prayer is that God would open your eyes to see that favor rests upon you as well!

Baker's Evangelical Dictionary of Biblical Theology defines *favor* as "gaining approval, acceptance, or special benefits or blessings." Interestingly enough, the word used for *grace* throughout the New Testament is *charis,* which literally translated means *favor. Grace* is often defined as "unmerited favor," or in other words, favor that we received by no doing of our own. This means the gospel message at its core is a message of divine favor! God so loved us that even while we were sinners He sent Jesus to die for our sins so we could receive the benefits of His resurrection life (John 3:16, Romans 5:8). This is good news because it clearly demonstrates that everyone has a measure of favor with God. He is very fond of each one of us.

Proverbs 16:15 tells us, "In the light of a king's face there is life, and his favor is like the clouds that bring the spring rain." The "light of a king's face" closely resembles Israel's famous benediction, first recorded in Numbers 6:25, that "God would cause the light of His face to shine upon us." This phrase in modern terms would translate something to the effect that God would smile upon us! This is a prayer asking for divine favor, that God would accept and bless His people. God's smile releases life into us. Favor is found in His face!

Stanza two of Proverbs 16:15 reveals the effect of divine favor operating in our lives: it is "like clouds that bring the spring rain." Ancient Israel was an agricultural society and therefore was highly dependent upon spring rain to fuel the economy. This verse is then relating that favor manifests as divine resource. Let me explain what this resourcing looks like by analyzing divine favor at play in the life of Jesus. He was born on earth to Mary and Joseph and was clearly set apart by God even in His infancy. However, it is very interesting that though He was the Messiah, he did not have the favor necessary to fulfill His earthly calling until He was thirty years old. Luke 2:52 tells us that the young boy, "Jesus increased in wisdom and in stature and in favor with God and man." I find this fascinating!

If Jesus needed favor with both God and man, so do we. When analyzing Jesus's earthly ministry, you come to realize the intense and hostile political, cultural, and spiritual climate that He engaged with. The wisdom He exuded in speaking to the very complicated socio-political dynamics at play is staggering (Matthew 5:41). The parables Jesus employed to expose the hypocrisy of the religious elite were jaw-dropping (Luke 10:5–37, 15:11–32). His charisma and healing power resounded through the Galilee like clarion calls drawing people to His message of the kingdom (Luke 5:15, 7:17). This is all evidence of God's favor at work through Jesus. However, we must realize that Jesus's ministry was not birthed overnight. His language and understanding weren't developed in a vacuum, but were derived from engaging with the grace of God through thirty years of silent preparation.

On the day of His baptism, God revealed His favor upon Jesus, publicly descending upon Him in the form of a dove. God then smiled and spoke publicly, "This is My beloved son in whom I am well pleased". This marked Jesus's transition from the season of preparation into days of fulfillment. Manifestations of power through Him began to systematically turn Israel upside down. It was not self-promotion or the promotion of man that catapulted

Jesus into national prominence—it was the light of God's smiling face manifesting through Jesus that accomplished this!. When Jesus arrived at this platform, He was poised to reveal what the Father had been cultivating in Him during the years of preparation. Jesus was fully resourced by divine favor to fulfill His call. This came in the form of anointing (Matthew 3:16), kingdom relationships (Matthew 10:2), and finances (Luke 8:1–3).

This pattern continues to repeat itself. Jesus tells his disciples early on in the gospel accounts that they will be "fishers of men" (Matthew 4:9). However, they did not have the favor necessary to complete this calling until after the day of Pentecost. On that day, the Spirit of God descended upon them in the upper room, and the Divine Presence began to exude from the disciples in great power. This quickly thrust them into a large ministry platform that systematically began to turn the Mediterranean world upside down. As with Jesus, this was not the fruit of self-promotion, but of divine favor. The manifest presence of God bestowed anointing upon these disciples and attracted people and financial resources (Acts 2:47, 4:34–35) that would help serve the vision they were tasked to fulfill.

I can attest to a similar dynamic in my own life. Favor has come primarily in the form of anointing, relational partnerships, and finances (I list these in order of importance). My unique call is to pioneer churches. This calling demands a specific anointing, a developed network of people willing to invest into the same vision, and a lot of money! No matter what the calling, the resources of heaven are vital to seeing the vision fulfilled. Divine favor is what attracts this!

As I stated at the beginning of this chapter, I used to have a very passive understanding of favor. This resulted in confusion in my prayer life. I would ask Him to bless my endeavors and do in my life what I saw Him doing in other people. This was good, but it lacked maturity. I knew God loved me and had manifold grace for me, but I didn't understand that I had *already* been given favor. This left me asking for more blessing while being a poor steward of what God had already bestowed. Our issue, then, is not whether we have divine favor or not, but how we steward the measure we have been given. If we are to grow in favor as Jesus did, we must first learn how to steward it well!

During this season of discovering the ways of divine favor, I had just begun my public preaching ministry. I was exploding with promise, as just a few months prior, God had brought me into a very powerful encounter that turned my world upside down. It was my "fisher of men" experience, where God came and spoke to me after many years in the wilderness. I finally understood and embraced my calling to pioneer churches as well as perform large-scale crusade evangelism. I was filled with promise and, for the first time in my life, absolutely convinced that I knew God's will for my life. This mountaintop experience had me ready to see the world change and this word come to pass, but what I ended up experiencing was a season of disillusionment.

Almost immediately, I began to experience sharp criticism, painful wounds, and church services where I was preaching to six people (including myself and the two people on the worship team). To say I was frustrated was an understatement! I had read stories of supernatural church growth and how divine blessing and favor would flood through a ministry, and it simply was not happening for me. I became disillusioned with what was and wasn't happening and convinced myself that the reason God wasn't moving was because of the church I was a part of. I began searching for a ministry to go join where "God would be free to move." My heart was not sour in this process; I was simply confused and unable to reconcile the promise God had put on my life with the reality of my circumstances. What I was unaware of was that though I had a promise from God, I didn't yet have the favor necessary to see the promise fulfilled. I was in a season of preparation, not fulfillment. This meant I had to accept the reality that growing in favor is a process. Jesus spent thirty years in hidden preparation. The disciples were tasked with three years of rigorous mentorship by our Lord. It would be a curious thing to expect anything different for ourselves! In His great kindness, God came to me in my disillusionment and began prodding me to seek out understanding of His favor. As I sought wisdom in this matter, He opened my eyes and began teaching me what good stewardship consists of.

The first step in faithful stewardship is a recognition that you have been given favor. It might not be like your neighbor's or best friend's favor, but as you are a child of God with an identity in Christ, it is a certainty that you have a measure of favor available to you! During this time, I was preaching to six people, experiencing sharp criticism, and wondering what on earth God was accomplishing through it! I felt as though I had no favor, but God began to open my eyes to what I'd been blind to. He began revealing that He loves to work inside out. His primary concern is the character development of the heart, and His secondary concern is how this is expressed in what we do and whom we serve.

He told me that He was giving me favor to learn patience. In other words, He was anointing me in that season not to grow a huge church and see the miraculous invade earth—but to cultivate the fruit of patience within my heart. This was not what I wanted to hear! He said all the frustration I was experiencing was my opportunity to learn to be patient, just like Jesus is patient, and that I had a choice to make. I could continue to whine and complain and try to change my circumstances, or I could choose to rejoice that God was using the circumstances I was in to transform my heart into the image of Jesus. I chose the latter and in so doing resolutely decided that my joy in life would be found in becoming like Jesus, not in my circumstances.

Practically speaking, God used a certain individual to cultivate patience in me. We were in a state of ongoing conflict and frustration, as we could not see eye to eye on a number of important topics. I left many meetings with this person feeling so offended and frustrated my head could explode. It was so difficult that at one point we had to bring in a mediator to help us communicate. The Lord clearly instructed me going forward that if I was serious about stewarding His favor and cultivating patience, I needed to get really excited about meeting with this individual. He told me to start rejoicing and thanking Him for all the patience He was growing in me as I would drive to these meetings. I found that as I began to do this, my perspective shifted drastically. Instead of feelings of dread, I would start to feel excited. Within a number of months, it was no longer an issue for me; God had changed my heart by the power of His grace! God taught me through this that He does not always desire to immediately change our adverse circumstances; instead, He uses them to change us!

The decision to find joy in becoming like Jesus has proved to be exceedingly fruitful because I have found that no matter the circumstance, there is always opportunity to become more like Christ. Recognizing and remaining in this truth are key to living as an overcomer. You become invincible to the schemes of hell because no matter what is or isn't happening, nothing can prevent you from becoming more like Jesus. This is the power of focusing on and rejoicing in the favor being given to you by God.

The first place to look when searching for the favor you're being given is inside. Focus on who God is forming you to be. Ask Him what fruit of the Holy Spirit He is bestowing favor to cultivate in this season, and then yield to the process. When the storms of life are raging, God often is granting favor to cultivate peace. When you are experiencing a very harsh relational dynamic, there is grace to grow in His kindness. In every situation you face in life, God will grant you the favor necessary not just to survive it, but to overcome and manifest the life of Jesus through it. This will result in your own personal well-being and also demonstrate faithful stewardship of God's favor.

God's secondary, external concern in regard to stewardship is your faithfulness to whom He has called you to serve. In this season, God had entrusted me with a very small group of people. He would often whisper to me, "Prepare now like you are speaking to thousands, and one day you will speak to thousands." I knew what He was getting at—He was asking me to give my whole heart, no matter the audience and no matter what they thought of me. I can honestly say I have poured my heart and passion into every sermon I have ever preached (and there were many awkwardly small nights)!

We are told not to despise small beginnings (Zechariah 4:10), and this, again, is an issue of stewardship. God was wanting to see if it was my love for people, or a desire for personal greatness that was motivating me in building the ministry. Whether we are building a ministry or a business, it is love that must be at the center of our pursuits. God trained me through humble circumstances to tap into the motivation of love. The process of growing in favor hinges upon our development in love. Love does not seek its own (1 Corinthians 13:5). If we are to use the favor we receive for the sake of those we serve, we must become holy, selfless love. This is what stewardship is all about. God divinely orchestrates circumstances where we are given opportunity after opportunity to grow up into love.

As I navigated the journey of learning faithful stewardship, I became aware it is not one devoid of pitfalls. I discerned two subtle influences that, if not recognized, will thwart us in our efforts to grow in favor. The first trap that must be identified is comparison. The parable of the talents depicted in Matthew 25:14–30 gives clear insight into the relationship between favor and comparison.

In this parable, a man is preparing to leave on a long journey, and so he distributes his possessions to his servants. Verse 15 records, "To one he gave five talents, to another two, and to another, one; *each according to his own ability.*" This may sound offensive at first reading, but something that must be recognized in regard to God's favor is that He does not distribute it the same way to everyone. All His children are loved equally, but some are given more favor than others.

This point hit home for me in 2013, while I was serving in Africa. I was in the back of a camion truck that literally had fifty people jammed into it. The space was so tight that my face was at most six inches from the face of an older woman next to me who had her grandson, named Samuel, sitting on her lap. For the next four or five hours, I shared this very intimate space with these two individuals. I have never been physically closer to a human being for so long a time in my life.

As we sat crammed together in the back of this truck, I felted prompted to pray for Samuel, and as I did, my heart started to break. It broke because I was forced, for multiple hours, to recognize that though I was sharing this intimate space with this African boy in a remote part of northern Mozambique, our lives could not be further apart. In a week's time, I would be on a flight to America in time to celebrate the holidays with my family, and he would be in a remote village in the bush of Africa. I began to process all the privilege, resource, education, freedom, and opportunity that I have in my life compared to this boy, simply because I was born to a family living in the United States of America. This isn't fair. I don't deserve these things, and I did nothing to earn this favor, yet God in His wisdom has chosen to bless me with it. The point I am trying to make is that there is favor I have been given that Samuel has not. This disparity is a fact of life. He would look at myself, or anyone living in America, and easily assess that, *materially speaking,* we have been given five talents.[9]

Though this is indeed isn't fair, I'd like to propose to you that in the end it doesn't matter how much favor you start with. In the conclusion of the parable of the talents, we are told how each of the servants went about stewarding the talents (favor) they had received. The Master arrived home, and the first two servants disclosed that they had doubled what they were given, making ten and four talents respectively. The master then revealed the reward of their good stewardship, and it is the exact same thing! He tells them both, "Well done, good and faithful slave. You were faithful with a few things, I will put you in charge of many things; enter into the *joy* of your master." Jesus made it very clear—in regard to favor, it does not matter what you start with; it's what you do with what you are given that matters most.

Whether you begin with much or with little, faithful stewardship will position you to see external increase and internal joy! Comparison seeks to derail us from this path by getting us offended or complacent. God has us each on our own journey, and no two paths are the same. If we despise what we've been given because we don't think it is enough, or applaud ourselves because of our relative abundance and do nothing with what God has graciously granted, we become the servant who hid his talent in the dirt. This servant saw no increase and received no joy. Partnering with comparison leads to tragic results.

In the aftermath of my season spent in Africa, I came home more aware than ever of the five talents I'd been given. Accepting this was very sobering for me. I confess openly that the more time I spend in the Global South, the more I am disturbed by the vast disparity I see between the material wealth of the West and the painful poverty of the South. This disturbance has forced me to deeply reflect upon the purpose favor is meant to fulfill and to deeply ponder the question, "Why have I been given it?" In this pursuit, I have resolutely come to believe that favor is given solely for the sake of those we are called to serve. We must recognize that the greater the favor, the greater the responsibility.

This leads us to the second pitfall on the path to good stewardship: self-promotion, or in other words, using divine favor for our own gain. Any resource given above and beyond the provision of our needs is intended by God to be a blessing to others. I see too many people I know and love miss out on the fullness of God's blessings because they fail to steward the blessing and influence they have been given well. Social media is an arena where I see this often. People will have large followings, amounting in many tens of thousands of followers, and nearly everything posted is about themselves. I am not saying this is inherently wrong, but that it is incomplete. What would happen if we used these media platforms to champion the marginalized? What would happen if we used our influence to cry out on behalf of the voiceless? What would result if we viewed the platforms we've been given as means to serve others and not ourselves?

These are mindsets and actions of a heart bent toward radical generosity. The generous know that God will give to us what He can get through us! When we are "clean pipes," free from the clogging scum of self-promotion, we are postured to grow in favor. God can't resist giving us more because He knows it will arrive at His intended target—the ones we are called to serve!

I wrestled with the temptation to compare and self-promote a lot in the early days starting in ministry, and to be honest, nothing has changed. These are ongoing battles that we will have to face as we continue to grow in favor. This is actually really exciting! If we recognize these opponents and arm ourselves for the fight, we will overcome, and increase will always be the inevitable result!

Most notable to that first season in ministry, I recognized the seductive voice of comparison was compelling me to run to a new circumstance "where the grass was greener" and I would have more favor. By His grace, I resisted this temptation, instead yielding to the stewardship process, and to my surprise, something amazing began to happen! The first change I noticed was internal: instead of being miserable, I found myself full of peace and joy *in the midst of the process.* This is a huge indicator for me that I am successfully abiding in God. I am by nature a forward thinker and have a tendency to "live in the future" with my thoughts and emotions. In doing this, I often outpace God, and this creates a dynamic where peace and joy are carrots dangled on a stick in front of me. I've found that when I recognize God's favor in a particular season and yield to His process of ongoing sanctification, I am given peace and joy. This was the internal outcome of stewarding the favor of God.

The external shift that took place is that God's favor began increasing upon my life and ministry. Particularly in the realm of preaching, I began to notice His wisdom exuding through me in a measure I had never previously experienced. This began to be confirmed by individuals within my ministry, and more and more feedback began to express a similar sentiment. The anointing of heaven is the greatest resource we will ever receive. The Holy Spirit is the source of all wisdom, and when He begins speaking into our endeavors, fruit is inevitable. Whether preaching a sermon, running a business, drafting a legislative bill, writing a teaching curriculum, preparing financials, or raising children, we need His anointing upon our lives.

I found that as His anointing began to increase upon my preaching, this attracted the next great resource of heaven: the people of God. He began to sovereignly bring the people through whom he would work to build what He was desiring to create, and I still to this day have no idea how it all took place. I have seen this trend continue for the last four years, and it never ceases to amaze me how God orchestrates connecting His people together.

Over the next eighteen months, I watched as God grew my very small young adult ministry into something substantial. People began having powerful experiences with God, and heart transformations were taking place. I was overjoyed and in awe and wonder as to how this ministry happened. This ministry, which was called Encounter Movement, was the first kingdom creation God produced through me. It was a seed of promise in my heart, and I watched God supernaturally birth and grow it under my stewardship. I loved these people more than I know how to describe.

During the year when the ministry experienced increase in presence and growth, the Lord began speaking to me about the next phase in my process of learning good stewardship. He told me, "Your first fruits will be holy unto the Lord. You're going to give Encounter away." These words stung me very deeply, and it was five months of processing before I could come to a place of accepting them. The thought of abandoning the ministry that I had poured my heart and soul into was almost too hard to bear. Sitting in the tension of that year was extremely uncomfortable, yet I knew that the favor He was granting me was to learn about His goodness in this time of sacrifice.

Through this, I learned an invaluable lesson about stewardship: we are not owners, but stewards of the artifacts God creates through us. Yes, I was the vessel that God used to birth this kingdom creation, but it belonged to Him. I had been wrestling with feelings of shame over the prospect of leaving, and so I fasted for an extended period, seeking clarity. At the end of this fast, God spoke clearly to me and told me, "You were anointed to birth this ministry, and now my anointing is lifting from you for this role. If you continue, it will bring about destruction. If you obey and surrender, I will raise up someone in your place." This was a hard pill to swallow, as it exposed that I saw myself as more important than I was, but it also liberated me to make a confident decision.

I realized that the favor in this season had changed. I was no longer anointed to grow that ministry, but to learn the sacrificial generosity of Christ. We must continually seek to understand the favor we are being given and then yield to it.

Four months after God spoke these words, I had my last Sunday and passed the ministry over to new leadership. That was one of the saddest nights of my life. Mostly because of how deeply I loved the people God had entrusted to my leadership, and also because of the pain of being misunderstood. Transition is very difficult in any organization, and my experience is that it is even more difficult in the church. This is because of how much love-equity is sowed into creating it. You are more than coworkers—you are family. I went out that night to a river by myself and wept for a very long time. I worshipped as I wept, and I told the Lord it was my joy to obey Him. He comforted me and assured my heart that He was good.

This was a painful experience for me, but looking back, I can tell you it accomplished so much. Laying down something so precious served to cleanse me from the scum of self-promotion. It created within me the ability to care for something intently without clasping too tightly for control. God's blessings are intended to bring us joy, not security. I learned this because I yielded to the favor He was giving me. He anointed me in that season to be transformed into the image of Jesus, particularly in regard to His generosity. This has since served me well.

In the wake of my releasing Encounter Movement, God released me to plant my now-current church, River House, in a different city. This was a really scary thought for me. Encounter was a part of a larger church that provided financial support and backing, making the process much simpler and more secure for me. Additionally, up until this point, my primary audience was young adults and college students, which made sense because I was only twenty-five at the time of leaving Encounter! For these reasons, starting a church that would be financially self-sustaining seemed like a mountain too big to climb. I was overwhelmed, worn out from the last three years of ministry that ended painfully, and deeply aware of my lack of experience pastoring and organizing a church.

I planned a trip to Southeast Asia[10] with a couple friends to fill the "in-between" space I would have transitioning from Encounter to the church plant. The purpose of the trip for me was to clear my mind and create some space for God to breathe fresh inspiration into me. My friend had connections to an orphanage that he had helped establish and we were going to visit. Besides this, our only other plan was to travel around the region by train. I arrived in Southeast Asia a couple weeks after my friends. They picked me up at four a.m. I was jet-lagged and hoping to find a bed to sleep in. One of them told me that we were going to go the slums later that morning to pray for some people. In my heart, I was annoyed; that was the last thing I wanted to do in the moment. My body was craving rest!

They let me go home, change my clothes, and lie down for a few hours, and then we were off into the helter-skelter busyness of the overcrowded city life. There were riots all throughout the city, and so with much caution, the national pastor who was hosting us took us to a small slum church so we could pray for some people. The first person I ever prayed for in Southeast Asia was an elderly woman who was crippled and lived on the street. She was carried in and sat on a chair. I motioned to my friend John to place his hand on her left knee, and I had my hand on her right kneecap. I began to pray a simple prayer of healing, and to my surprise, her knee literally "popped" in my hand. She stood up and began walking. I was amazed but then was quickly ushered to pray for someone else. In a short time, the church became flooded with people piling in from the street. I found out later that this was due to the testimony of the once-crippled woman walking up and down the street telling all her neighbors that Jesus had healed her!

I continued ministering for the next nine to ten hours as the pastors were taking us from church to church, and God continued extending His hand to heal. The night ended in a very, very small church in a slum where the manifest glory of God invaded. People began waking the sick and the crippled up out of bed and bringing them into the church. There was a crowd that formed around the building that made it impossible for me to get out. My friend on the outside of the building marveled that it was like watching the gospels play out in front of His eyes. One of the national pastors commented that he thought people were going to tear a hole in the roof to get people down for prayer! God touched many people that night, and I have since returned back and heard people testify to what God did for them on that evening.

The next day, I was sitting at the dinner table with the pastor who had escorted us around the city. He described to me how he had never seen anything quite like what happened that night and then began to tell me a story. He said there was a man of God who had been coming for decades doing crusades in their region but two years prior had passed away. They had been praying to God to send someone in his stead that could re-dig the well and begin once again the work of crusade evangelism. He then looked at me and asked me to please pray about returning to do a crusade the next year.

I was speechless and in awe of God. "And suddenly" His word over my life that I would build His church and perform crusade evangelism was beginning to come to fruition. I have heard it said that one day of favor is better than a thousand days of labor. I can personally attest to the validity of this statement! During my first day in Southeast Asia, God's favor showered upon me, and He began a work that I thought would have taken a decade to accomplish. *I stress that this all took place because of God's favor.* His manifest presence resting upon me is what opened the door for this work to begin. I could not have manipulated it into existence if I tried with all my might. His anointing resting upon me again attracted the people I would need to partner with to see this vision come to pass. My obedience to God in laying down Encounter Movement is what led me to Southeast Asia and positioned me to receive what God was intending to bless me with. Failing to do so would have limited the measure of favor on my life, not because God didn't desire to give more, but because I was not mature enough to handle it. Obedience does not always feel good in the moment, but God will always use it to create good!

On my plane ride home from Southeast Asia, I was praying to God, asking Him what on earth was happening. I had a small church of ten people in Boise, Idaho, named River House, and now a ministry being birthed across the world in Asia. I had no idea how these two things fit together, no idea how these ventures would be funded, and no idea how I would be successful at either one of them. The only thing I was sure of was that I was growing in favor. I was witnessing God moving through me in ways that only years earlier had seemed out of reach. Even so, I could have never imagined all that would take place in the days that followed.

CHAPTER EIGHT

Kingdom Fruitfulness

And the Father's will is that you bear much fruit.

———

JOHN 15:8

I BEGAN THIS WORK BY STATING THAT THE HIGHEST CALL OF GOD upon His image-bearers is to create kingdom artifacts that demonstrate the fulfillment of the Lord's prayer, "Thy kingdom come and Thy will be done on Earth as it is in heaven." I have since shared the major lessons learned in both the breaking and building seasons of the last ten years of my life. What I will now describe are the consequences that resulted from all of this. God knows the plans that He has for us, and they are good. Every lesson He teaches us is laced with purpose. He is molding each of us into a vessel fit for honorable use (2 Timothy 2:20–21).

We are created to live life co-laboring with God. We know when this is taking place when the "Only God" factor is evident. This is referring to a quality of life that far exceeds our own abilities, skill sets, and intellect and is therefore supernaturally (above the natural limitations of our humanity) fruitful. This is God's will for our lives. He created us to fulfill this purpose on earth. We were created to co-create the kingdom on earth with Him.

River House is the name of a kingdom creation that God, myself, and a community of people are pioneering together. River House is both a divine and a human creation. It is highly evident that this is the case. God and this community have partnered together, and we are seeing the kingdom of God break into earth as a result. I want to share some stories that help bring this to life.

River House began with ten people who met in a backyard in June of 2016. We had no backing, no money, no name, no building, and a lot of faith. I was honestly really overwhelmed because in a really deep sense I had no idea what to do. One of the scariest parts of this season was all the "wise" voices that communicated the concerns of church-planting. I found there was a lot of negativity associated with pioneering ministry, backed by many "horror stories" of failure and disappointment. I had people suggest lots of ideas of what I should do if I wanted to be successful. Very little of this was helpful.

When I would go to the Lord, He repeatedly would tell me the same thing: "All I need you to do is listen to My voice and obey Me. I will build My church." And so that's what we did. My motto that I told everyone in those early days is that we were going to do this in such a way that if God didn't show up, the church wasn't going to work. Nothing has changed in this regard. In practical terms, this looked like two things. First, we chose the path of financial dependence—we have still, to this day, never asked for money outside of the church tithes. Second, we don't advertise. Leonard Ravenhill said, "You never have to advertise a fire. You don't have to advertise it in the newspaper, forget it. You let the glory of the Lord fill the temple; people will come from hundreds of miles."[11] Our motivation in this was to position ourselves to know if God was truly in this or not. I would rather have no ministry at all than one that is being propped up by my efforts and self-promotion tactics.

We opened up our Sunday evening prayer and worship meeting in August of 2016 and have been in awe ever since at God's working. The creative vibration of God started stirring over the waters of our community, and supernatural fruitfulness ensued. Within two months, we had outgrown two small spaces we rented and settled into a church building that we could use on Sunday evenings. By the end of the year, we had grown to roughly seventy-five people and were so thankful.

Our leadership team had our end-of-the-year meeting in December and decided that we needed to start searching for a part-time children's pastor. Within a week, I received a call saying there was a candidate from out of state we should consider. He was a friend of a friend and currently serving as the children's pastor of a mega-church in Arizona. I asked, "Why on earth would he want to come work part time in a church of seventy-five people?" I was told to just call him.

I didn't call him for weeks because I was insecure about the thought. This guy had seven hundred children in his ministry, and River House as a whole was a tenth that size. I was driving down the road one day, in the middle of a fast, and the Lord spoke to me and said, "Call him tomorrow." I try to be a faithful servant, so I obeyed despite my concerns!

I cringed as Jamey, the children's pastor, answered the phone, as I fully expected a very awkward conversation to ensue. Instead, he began to tell me a story that blew my mind. He told me that six months prior, God spoke to him one morning and told him to prepare himself to leave the church he was at. Over the next six months, he had been seeking God in prayer as to where he was to go. He naturally thought it would be back home to the Midwest, but one day while he was in prayer, God flashed across his mind's eye two friends—Missy and Sarah—whom he had gone to college with twenty years prior and who now both lived in the Boise area. He knew then God was calling him to move to Boise, a place he had never been in his life! He reached out to them and asked them if they knew of any churches looking for a children's pastor. They told him about River House and said they didn't know if we were looking or not but, they would find out.

Jamey then continued by telling me that in the time since talking to Missy and Sarah, he had gotten onto the website and begun listening to the podcast. He told me that he had been praying for twenty years for a church that embodied the vision we were pursuing. He said all that he wanted was a spiritual environment that resonated with his heart—that he did not care about church size, financial compensation, or prestige—that whether I was interested or not, he would be honored to come and serve the vision of River House. Jamey then added that he and his family were in a middle of a twenty-one-day fast (which I was on as well) praying specifically over coming to River House.

I was in shock and couldn't help but think, *There is no way on earth he knows how small of a church we are, and there is no way he knows I'm only twenty-six!* We continued chatting, and I explained the church size and that I could only pay someone a part-time salary (which I knew would be insufficient to provide for his wife and two kids). His story didn't change at this; he meant what he had said. We prayed, connected powerfully, and then hung up the phone.

Almost immediately, I remembered that my mother, our family pastor, was landing in Phoenix (where Jamey lived) that same evening through a random series of events. I consulted my leadership team, and we set up an impromptu interview on the spot. Within three weeks, we had made an offer, and Jamey accepted. God had provided a children's pastor.

Five months later, he arrived with his beautiful family, and God worked wonders in providing for them. They were believing for a home in the countryside for eight hundred dollars a month (which is impossible) and couldn't find anything remotely close to this. One night, Jamey had a dream that led him to a road sign with the name "Beacon Light" on it. At one point, he came to a house that was near a horse stable. He called his realtor and described exactly what he had seen in the dream. The realtor informed him that there was indeed a road called Beacon Light and proceeded to get in the car and explore. She ended up stumbling upon a small country house, just down the road from a horse stable, that was for rent at eight hundred dollars a month! God is good. If that's not enough, a month after they arrived, a car was dropped off at their front doorstep with a bow on it from an anonymous source. Where God guides, God provides!

On Jamey's first Sunday, I was chatting with him post-service and asked what it was like finally being at River House. He told me, "It's strange—I've been praying for this for twenty years." This stopped me in my tracks. I was six years old when those prayers began. "Only God!"

I'm being honest when I tell you that these types of stories are the norm for River House, not the exception. A few weeks after Jamey arrived, we had a very strange Sunday gathering. Only minutes before service was scheduled to begin, the power in the building completely shut off, and it remained dark in the building until the closing prayer! At the end of service, I noticed an African American man whom I had never seen before chatting with some people. They called me over and said, "Jordan, you need to hear this story!"

This man, Sherrod, began telling me that he had just moved to Boise that week. He said that a number of months earlier, he had had a dream where he was in his car driving to Boise. In the dream, when he got to Boise, he walked into a building that was completely dark. He ran into a girl named Hayli that he knew in college (and hadn't seen in years), but besides that recognized no one else. He said throughout the whole dream, the place was dark, but he knew something very powerful was taking place in the people in the building. He knew that people were being equipped to go out and change the world. You can imagine his surprise when he walked into our church, which was completely dark because of the power outage, and as he walked into the sanctuary, he ran into Hayli (who is a core member of River House). His dream was about our church family. "Only God!"

I share these stories because they exemplify the way in which God is growing our church. These are things that I could never conjure up if I tried for a hundred years, and yet they are happening on a regular basis. We have had many stories already of people moving from other states to come and join our community. At our one-year birthday service, we had two girls fly from Virginia to Idaho, testifying that the podcast had changed their lives and they wanted to come experience River House in person. Ravenhill's words have resoundingly rung true: people have come from hundreds of miles to see the glory of God manifest in our community. Every time these "Only God" stories happen, they don't just make us feel good, but they also boost the faith of the congregation. We are all convinced that God is at work. He is faithfully building His church.

To stress this further, what we have seen God accomplish in Southeast Asia has been equally, if not more, remarkable. Through partnership with local leadership, we are witnessing the momentum of God birth a beautiful movement in that land. A men's and women's biblical seminary has been created, a pastoral network pioneered, and crusade evangelism effectively used to invigorate and refresh churches and local leaders. A long-term kingdom strategy in its fruitful infancy has been birthed. It has taken my breath away. I could not have imagined this all taking place in ten years, much less in eighteen months. We have heard testimonies that bear a striking resemblance to what we are seeing in Boise. People are having supernatural experiences that are confirming the validity of God's movement through our ministry engagement.

We partnered in putting on a ministry crusade in Southeast Asia in July of 2017. We had no idea what to expect, and many of the local leaders were worried because of my age. What resulted was very remarkable, as over the three days, we had between two and three thousand in attendance. In particular, the last night was so crowded that the stage had to be used to seat people. God was ministering powerfully, bringing conviction, repentance, and many dozens of testimonies of supernatural healing. Months later, one of the leading pastors in the region confessed that they were all shocked at how fruitful the event was. He told me, "No one knows who you are in this city. We cannot figure out why so many came. Only a month before you were here, we had a very prominent minister come to our city and put on a very expensive crusade, and almost nobody came. It was a huge flop. Many people have been asking us what we have done to achieve such success, and we tell them we do not know. All we did is pray, and God brought the people." I feel like I am repeating myself, but there it is again: "Only God." I'm not able to make this stuff up!

Through this process, my mind has been renewed about what it means to pioneer churches and ministry. The stories of striving, deep disappointment, and financial lack are the fruit of operating out of independence, not God's intended plan for building His church. The last two years have been very difficult, requiring a lot of work and a fair share of heartache, yet I can resolutely testify that the momentum of God has been extraordinary. We have never lacked. Our finances have been remarkable. Our growth has been tremendous, the testimonies of transformation abundant.

God's promise is that He will build His church and the gates of hell will not prevail (Matthew 16:18). This is true! God is a genius. He knows how to make a church thrive. I saw this birth from the lessons I have described in the previous chapter of this book—the breaking of independence, uprooting of shame, revelation of my belovedness, art of prayer, stewardship of favor, and dual identity of servant and son. All of this played a significant role in the creation of these kingdom artifacts. God knows what He is doing in the journey He is leading us on.

I want to emphasize that though I am experiencing fruitfulness, I have not arrived to a place of "Christian mastery." This is an esoteric myth that is bound to lead to disillusionment. Our tendency is to believe we are headed toward an earthly destination in our walks with Jesus where our suffering turns to perfect joy, fruitfulness abounds, and success is achieved. This is not the case. There are mountains beyond mountains in the climb of discipleship. There is always a journey ahead of us (Luke 24:28). To make it very clear, everything I have shared throughout this book are truths I am still learning to embody more and more deeply. The Word becoming flesh in us is a process of lifelong development.

My call is to create and pioneer churches, but yours may be to create a family as a stay-at-home mom, or to own a small business, or to be a teacher, or to work in corporate America. The beautiful thing is that building the kingdom encompasses all of this. The "Only God" factor is available to all God's children and to any calling. I mentor a young man who has a call to business and a burning passion for the things of God. When I met him, he was burdened over how to reconcile these two things. He was struggling over the question of whether he should quit business to go into youth ministry. It's been a joy to witness God liberate him and disciple him into the calling he's been given to bring heaven to business. It is a joy to watch him fight to prioritize prayer in the demands of the high-paced business world. A privilege to witness him repent from independence, pride, and idolatry as he allows the love of God to permeate and sanctify his heart. The fruit of this has been extraordinary. God is filling him with dreams of what it looks like to create heavenly business models that usher His kingdom into our city. What is taking place in and through him has left many saying, "Only God!" This is what he was created to do!

The truth is that we all have heavenly blueprints embedded within our hearts, and when we do the work of abiding in God, He breathes them into life. The journey is difficult, full of painful lessons, and incredibly costly, but in the end, it is God's way alone that leads to true fruitfulness and fulfillment. Taking the road less traveled, the one marked by self-emptying and dying to self, is what prepares us for all of this.

John Maxwell often reiterates, "Everything rises and falls on leadership."[12] I have experientially found this to be true, as it is leadership that most influences the culture of any organization, community, family, or church. To remind you, culture is what humans make of the world, in both senses. In other words, it is the physical creations we make and how we make sense of what they mean. A simple example of this would be a plate of bacon and eggs that I make for a guest staying at my home. Materially speaking, I created breakfast; yet if I did it with a heart of kindness, the meaning attached to this act was love. Therefore, the result of this small act is a beautiful creation called a relationship! This is how culture is created; it's what we make out of the world we have been given.

When we are creating something, we create out of who we are. More simply put, our creations express something about ourselves. I recently took my church staff to a pottery shop to paint an item of our choosing. It was fascinating to see how each person's creation matched his or her personality so intricately. Creativity in essence is an act of self-disclosure. Therefore, culture is an expression of the human beings that have created it.

Culture is the driving force of any family, community, or organization, though it is often subconscious in its working. Culture is like the deep ocean currents that carry ships long distances without ever being seen. The more that God is woven into a culture, the more life, hope, and momentum will be evident. He is the Creative Force of the universe, and letting Him loose to operate through us will result in unimaginable fruitfulness.

Practically speaking, culture is created through our words and actions. Everything we do or say carries great implications and causes a ripple effect in our lives. For example, I imagine every person reading this has been adversely affected by divorce in one way or another. You may have been two, or three, or four relationships away from it, but it still affected you. This is because we are all deeply interconnected. One horrible decision impacts at best hundreds, if not thousands of people. The same is true of the opposite.

Our actions are all motivated by either love or fear. Anything done in love, which is derived from God, will ultimately produce goodness and redemption in the earth. It will create a ripple effect of righteousness that brings in its wake the kingdom of God. This is how culture is created! We speak the words of God and do the works of God, and He creates the culture of the kingdom through us. We must recognize that we are called to preach the gospel of the kingdom to the world, not just the salvation message. Leading people to the

Lord is an incredible experience, but our calling is so much more than this! We are called to co-create the culture of heaven through every word and action we make.

Jesus modeled this everywhere He went. His words and actions were all prophetic messages that opened a door for people to come into the kingdom. When I say prophetic messages, I am describing a dynamic where what Jesus created both resonated with and disturbed the presiding cultural norms. An example of this would be how He instructed the Jews to engage with Roman soldiers. The Romans were legally empowered to subject the Jews to carry their armor for one mile whenever they wished. I'm sure this act infuriated the Jewish people, making them feel like they were beasts of burden. Jesus spoke directly to this messy dynamic in such a way that He ushered in the kingdom. He said, "And if anyone forces you to go one mile, go with them two" (Matthew 5:21). Recognize the wisdom of these words! Jesus was creating culture!

Jesus's message to carry the Roman's armor two miles spoke powerfully into the conscience of the Jews listening to His words. It resonated with them because it offered them a way to protest and keep their dignity in the face of being a subject people group. Carrying the armor two miles spoke a powerful, nonverbal, and nonviolent message: "Though you subject me to ill-treatment, I am not your slave and will not passively submit to injustice." Though empowering, this was disturbing because it critiqued the mindsets of both the victim and the zealot. The kingdom response, to carry the armor two miles, revoked the right to wallow in self-pity, as well as to violently revolt. Jesus's words were prophetic—they both resonated with and disturbed the people of Israel with the message of the kingdom!

As Christians, we are all facing similar dynamics every day. God sends us each into different subcultures of society that are full of messy situations! We are there because He is desiring to use our words and actions to show people an alternative way to engage with life—the way of the kingdom! When we are connected to Jesus, His wisdom and creativity will flow through our words and actions, and we will become living prophetic messages of the kingdom to the world, just like Jesus!

This is why the deconstruction process is so vital: it is the death of the fleshly, carnal thoughts and desires that gives God access to our whole beings and our every decision. Before we die to self, all that our words and actions create will be full of self. These creations, and the culture they produce, may be full of good intentions, but ultimately, everything is judged according to its source. If it comes from self, it is inherently selfish and will bring no true transformation to the earth. Yet if it originates in God, it won't just impact earth, but will actually abide forever because it is an expression of the Eternal One (John 15:16).

One of the things I am most thankful for is how God stripped away insecurity from my heart. If I was the person on the inside today that I was seven years ago, I would be living in personal turmoil, unable to cope with my shame, and would be blindly sowing insecurity and fear into the culture of River House through my words and actions. This would then infect River House and hinder the fullness of what God is desiring to accomplish. I am not saying that God would not get His will accomplished, but I am stating that it would not be happening through me if I was still living in the performance paradigm of insecurity, shame, and pride. The sobering and inspiring reality is that God has entrusted us with responsibility in the relationship of building His kingdom on earth. It is foolish to think that our unwillingness to yield to the Potter's hands will have no effect upon His will being accomplished in our lives.

In my experience, insecurity in leadership manifests in some very obvious and harmful ways, and if it is not recognized, it can lead to very destructive consequences. Raising up powerful people is the goal of leadership, yet insecurity undermines and sabotages this from the start. When I say "powerful people," I am referring to individuals that are equipped to lead and create healthy culture. They are not leeches along for the ride, but gifted, capable, and secure individuals *who do not need you* to function and be successful. Families and organizations function best when love is the motivating factor in leadership; this implies that we submit to leadership because *we want to!* Jesus is not an authoritarian who demands our allegiance but a humble leader who wins our hearts and helps us thrive in life. Our leadership should be no different. It is the ultimate act of servanthood, where we create a space for those we lead to take risks in expressing themselves and fulfilling their callings in a context of safety where they are believed in, protected, and loved. People should absolutely love being under our leadership. They should reckon it a precious gift from God. This is evidence that we are leading like Christ.

When we operate out of insecurity, thereby creating a culture influenced by shame, performance, and self, what I just described will be impossible to produce. In an insecure paradigm, powerful individuals may come, but they will eventually leave because they will be viewed as subtle threats in all their giftedness. Feeling threatened by those you lead is clear evidence that insecurity is at work. It is easy to justify this threat under many guises, but what it all boils down to is fear and self-protection.

God places authority on us in leadership to make those we lead better than ourselves. That statement is one of the scariest truths that I wrestle with on a regular basis. I constantly place this question in front of me: "Do I have the courage to humble myself to the point that I allow others to truly outshine and outgrow me?" This is the task I've been given from the Lord, and I am on the journey to fulfilling it. The fear that rises as I ponder this question is that of obscurity. I want my life to matter. As humans, our fleshly tendency is to fear change and the unknown and instead try to control situations in pursuit of security. This tendency gets exposed in the dying process. We come through the refining fire and find our controlling grip is not as strong as it once was.

There are a number of practices that the Lord has instructed me to employ in my leadership that have served to deepen my growth in humility and dependence in the midst of the fruitfulness I've been experiencing. These practices in truth consist of prophetic words and actions that both resonate with and disturb me with the message of the kingdom. Funnily enough, I have found that they do the same thing to the whole church! These practices have had profound impact on the culture of River House and demonstrate practically how the kingdom has infused itself into the DNA of our community. I will highlight two of these practices below.

One is inviting guest ministers who have different perspectives from mine to come and minister at River House. This may sound irreproducible outside of a church setting, but the principle isn't. Part of leading powerful people is that there must be room for differing opinions and perspectives. As it pertains to leading the church, whenever God instructs me to bring in a speaker, He tells me to hand over the reins and let Him lead through the guest minister. I was not prepared for how scary this would be! There have been times when I could sense people in my congregation getting offended and uncomfortable, and there was nothing I could do. This is what disturbance looks like!

There was one time in particular when I literally thought I had destroyed the church. What was happening on stage violated my ministry paradigm. It was weird. It was provocative. I was sure that many people were going to leave. I sat in the front row pondering how I could shut the PA system off, or cause a power outage, or somehow save what was happening, and then the Lord met me with His peace. He assured me that I could trust Him to build His church.

He spoke to me the week following this experience and told me I needed to teach the church how to honor those with different experiences, beliefs, and perspectives if we wanted to be a kingdom people. I preached this message the following week and felt the church resonate deeply with the challenge. Within two months of the weird night, the church had doubled yet again. However, more importantly, I noticed we possessed a greater ability to recognize the person of Jesus at work in our midst. The prophetic act of letting go of control and empowering an outside perspective forced us to recognize that the way we do church is not the only way. It worked to break the walls of our box down so we could experience God in more of His fullness. Personally speaking, this act of letting go taught me that it is God who builds His church, and my job is to let Him have His way, no matter how uncomfortable it makes me. It exposed how uncomfortable I am when I am not in control, which served to draw me into a deeper place of surrender. Emptying of self is not an overnight affair. The implications of this act have created and continue to create the culture of the kingdom within our community and in my own heart. Our words and actions have profound implications when they originate in God!

Another leadership practice that I think is even more unsettling is what Craig Groeschel defines as "delegating authority."[13] He instructs that we are to delegate authority, and not just responsibility, to those that we lead. Delegating responsibility creates followers, while granting authority is what produces leaders. I heard him share this via podcast years ago, but I never realized how messy and vulnerable this would be in reality! At River House, we are pursuing a church model of simplicity and mission. We don't have many ministries outside of Sundays because our goal is for people to live the gospel out throughout the week. Our only midweek ministry is called "revival groups," which are in essence small churches that are tasked with expressing the gospel in the unique subcultures of our city. These groups are led by powerful individuals who have been given authority to create these missional house-church cultures.

Where vulnerability comes in this that I literally have no control over what is taking place in these. Revival groups are given oversight by our family pastor, and we seek to pastor the leaders well, but ultimately they have been given authority. This is so good and also scary! What if the groups fail? What if groups grow and succeed and become their own churches? What if the leaders do or say something I don't approve of? These are all questions that I could let haunt me, but I don't because God has been preparing me for this. He taught me how to dig for understanding in times of fear and uproot its lies many years ago. I use this tool often. The truth is that God is leading River House. He is bigger than the messes we make, and He will build His church, His way. This posture of leading is risky, but it produces powerful leaders who will change the world, whether within River House or off pioneering their own works. My goal is to lead on the cutting edge. This is when one step further would mean chaos and one step back would be overly structured. This is the way of the kingdom!

This has meant embracing a posture of vulnerability far beyond what I am comfortable with. This has meant sleepless nights wrestling with my fear and insecurity when they get pulled up from the highs and lows of ministry. This all continues to push me deeper into the heart of Jesus. I've learned that there is no security in what God has called us to do; we find it only in walking closely with Jesus. Leadership isn't about your own personal security; it's about forfeiting it and laying your life down for other people. There is no way around this truth. Leadership in any form and context is designed to be an act of pure love.

It takes great courage to do this. Only the courageous will create things of great value and yet steward them without control. Only the courageous will lead powerful people and rejoice exceedingly in their exalting. We will find this courage when we know how loved we are. Many days throughout each week, the Lord reminds me that I belong to Him. I wear a necklace with the words "He's Mine" etched into it. It's who I am, and all this fruitfulness is flowing from that simple revelation of the Lion of Judah roaring over me.

I pray I have made it clear that this whole book is deeply interconnected. The pain and suffering are in no way disconnected from the joy and fruitfulness. The cries of agony were the seeds that sprouted into shouts of joy. I've tried to be as honest as possible and fully disclose both the breaking and the building processes, so that you may be equipped to wholeheartedly say yes to God.

This *yes* will hurt you deeply. It will cost you everything. Seriously. It will cost you things that you can't equate right now. It will mean painful disillusionment and many sleepless nights. It will evoke tears you didn't know you could cry. And yet, exceedingly and abundantly, it is worth it. A thousand times over, it is worth it. As I write this, I am twenty-seven years old, and I'm not exaggerating when I tell you I have seen God do more than I ever thought I would see in my whole life. Perhaps I was a shallow dreamer, but I don't think that's the case.

The Father's desire is that we bear much fruit. This fruit is eternal. It abides into the life beyond. Victor Frankl identified through his writings that "the chief desire of man is not pleasure, but meaning."[14] This is the deep craving of the human soul.

There was a particularly painful evening many years ago when I was desiring to give up on my faith and quit. The Lord was asking me to continue in faith and obedience, and I didn't want to do it. I was on a walk pondering what to do, and suddenly these words erupted from within me. I cried out, "God, I will keep going, and I'm not going to quit, but this is what I ask of you! On the day I die, in the moment when I breathe my last breath, let me do so in the peace of knowing that I gave everything and lived my life to the fullest. If you promise me this, I will never quit."

What I was attempting to express in that moment was my desire for a life of meaning, and consequently one devoid of regret. I'm certain that when we stand before the face of the Living God, there will be no remorse in our hearts over anything we gave to Him in this life. What we will regret is everything we kept from Jesus. I imagine it will be pure horror to recognize the immense beauty, meaning, and purpose that we forfeited in our puny self-preservation efforts. We were made for something extraordinary.

Jesus showed us the path to guaranteed fulfillment. It is the road of discipleship, and its central component is a cross. Embrace this awesome gift and let it accomplish its intent. Write the rights of your life away through surrender of your whole self. You will never regret this.

I pray that this little story from my little life in some way inspires you to offer something more to Jesus. I beg you, give Him your time. Offer Him your best. Yield to Him in all His fullness and allow Him His way in you. You were created to be an instrument of creative genius in the hands of an endlessly kind, beautiful, and humble King. We are all waiting for what you were destined to create.

ENDNOTES

1   Crouch, Andy. "The Definition of Culture." Lecture. 2014. Accessed February 2018. Christianitytoday.com.

For a more thorough explanation of Ken Myer's definition, listen to Andy Crouch's video "The Definition of Culture." Additionally, Andy's work *Culture Making* is a profound work that captures the power human creativity plays in discovering a life of deep meaning.

2   Tozer, A. W., and Ravi Zacharias. *The Radical Cross*. Chicago: Moody Publishers, 2015, page 73–74.

3   On the "dark night of the soul": Song of Solomon 5:6–16 depicts imagery of the bride who opens her heart to her beloved and then in dismay discovers his absence. She is then struck and wounded as she searches for him. In this place of pain, crisis, and lovesickness, she is asked, "What kind of beloved is your beloved?" This is the bride's testing, which becomes a sacred opportunity for her to profess her love of the bridegroom despite his apparent desertion. Her confession of love in this dark place leads to a deeper revelation of intimacy in the chapters that follow.

In a similar vein, in Genesis 15, Abraham goes through a literal dark night of the soul, where "terror and great darkness" fall upon him. The patriarch of Israel is confronted with the pain his people will have to endure in Egypt, and he is left to sit in the darkness alone. It is in the shade of this terror-filled night that God appears through a flaming torch and enters into a covenant with Abraham.

In both cases, the principle is evident that the dark night of the soul prepares the man or woman of God to enter more deeply into union with the Holy One.

4   Tozer, page 25.

5   In my personal experience of the Global South, which includes time in South America, Africa, and Asia, I have been continually astounded by how "normal" church in these regions would be deemed charismatic in the North American context. This is due to the wide acceptance of the activity of the Holy Spirit in their churches. In my experience within these regions, I have repeatedly found that dreams, visions, spiritual warfare, and healing miracles are common happenings in the lives of common believers. The Lord discipled me through what I have witnessed and opened my eyes to much I was unaware was possible. The operation of the gifts of the Holy Spirit in the Global South is widespread and undeniable; statistically speaking, it has led to the fulfillment of the Great Commission in unprecedented scale. I believe Western Christianity has much to learn from what the Church of the South has to say to us, particularly in regard to a resurgence of the power of God expressed in our churches. Yet for this to take place, we must become poor in spirit and posture our hearts to learn from our brothers and sisters.

6   For more information on the life and ministry of Heidi Baker, I recommend reading her work *There Is Always Enough*. Chapter 9 is entitled "All Fruitfulness Flows from Intimacy," and in context of the revival God has used her to lead, its implications are profound. There is much to glean from this very humble and powerful woman of God.

7   Guyon, Jeanne Marie Bouvier de La Motte. *Experiencing the Depths of Jesus Christ*. Beaumont, Texas: SeedSowers, 1996, page 57.

8   The art of prayer is a lifelong process of learning. I am a beginner on this journey and very eager to discover more. Resources I highly recommend are Jeanne Guyon's *Experiencing the Depths of Jesus Christ*, Richard Foster's *Prayer: Finding the Heart's True Home*, Norman Grubb's work *Rees Howells: Intercessor*, and Andrew Murray's *Abide in Christ*. These each offer a unique and profound perspective on the life of prayer.

9   I want to specify that I'm not advocating for a white savior/superiority complex in regard to Western relation to the Global South. In this example, I was intentionally using the contrast of material wealth, resource, and privilege as an example that demonstrates the disparity of resource distribution. I

could spend many pages describing the spiritual treasures that these cultures have, compared to the United States. Most notably on the topic of joy. I have experienced greater joy amongst the poor than I ever have amongst the wealthy. In this regard, we have much to learn. However, I chose not to use that example because it can be difficult to quantify and assign quality to immaterial things like emotions. Generally speaking, you have to experience the beauty of these cultures to recognize the poverty of our own in many regards. What I am getting at is that in some ways the United States has only one talent, while the Global South has five (and vice versa). Comparison is a thief; we must resist its influence and recognize that we all have something to offer one another. God distributes His favor uniquely, person to person and culture to culture. We all express a small portion of His manifold nature. If we all become good stewards, all will benefit.

10 I have chosen not to disclose the exact nation and location out of desire to protect the integrity of the work taking place in this region where the gospel is often under fire.

11 Ravenhill, Leonard. "Weeping Between the Porch and the Altar." Speech. 1994. Accessed February 2018. www.ravenhill.org.

12 Maxwell, John C. *Developing the Leader Within You*. HarperCollins Christian Publishing, 2018.

13 For more from Craig Groeschel, visit https://www.life.church/leadershippodcast/ to access his monthly podcast. His wisdom in the realm of leadership is a gift to the Body of Christ as a whole.

14 Miller, Donald. *Building a Storybrand: Clarify Your Message So Customers Will Listen*. New York: HarperCollins Leadership, an imprint of HarperCollins, 2017, page 4.

Miller penned the quoted statement in summary of Frankl's work *Man's Search for Meaning*, Beacon Press, 2006.

CPSIA information can be obtained
at www.ICGtesting.com
Printed in the USA
BVHW031402020119
536792BV00003B/55/P